REALITY IS A MATTER OF THE HEAD

how happiness works

why you don't implement your knowledge

and what your mind has to do with it

by

Jan Niklas Helbig

I translated it myself (and with the help of Google Translate). I'm sorry if you find spelling mistakes.

CONTENTS

ABOUT THE BOOK

or useless drivel from the author, which hardly interests anyone anyway, but somehow belongs to it

This book is the result of a ten-year and intensive journey through the world of thoughts and behaviors, driven by curiosity and the hunt for knowledge.

Countless books and documentaries, literature on philosophy from antiquity, from the Far East or the newest psychology. Discussions with the homeless, as well as with millionaires, psychologists, "coaches" and specialist trainers; always looking for knowledge. This hunt for the only true truth (if there was one) was and is the top priority of this book.

But to be honest, I wrote it primarily for myself

so that I can help myself and don't forget the knowledge. Because there was a time when I felt overwhelmed, helpless and torn out of the security of
childhood. Suddenly I was in life and the world,
which usually always stopped behind the horizon,
started right there. And it wasn't just the world
out there: everything I thought I knew, what I was,
what I be or what I believed sank into doubt. I was
looking for support and security, something that
strengthens me, that makes me happy - until I realized that I am responsible of myself. I can no longer
blame anyone.

Since I wrote the book (originally) for myself,
the source information or a professional expression
was not very important to me. Because the knowledge and the resulting knowledge have helped me
enormously, maybe it could also help other people.
I am also aware that I cannot help everyone, but if it
can help someone, it has already paid off.

INTRODUCTION

et's say: You read a sentence, it clicks and all your worries, needs and fears disappear. Ideally, all of your problems will fade away and life will be easy and harmonious. You implement your goals and everything succeeds. The dark veil of uncertainty and doubt dissolve, like the dark at dawn; all that remains is confidence and drive. A deep certainty that everything will be fine, that everything will work out. That the efforts are worthwhile. The daily struggle pays off.

This certainty would be awesome. But what keeps you from being like this? Is it external influences or are you responsible yourself? Do you think that inner stability comes from external circumstances or from yourself? And what does it mean to be happy? Does that mean having no problems or staying more impartial? Should I pursue goals or should I rather enjoy the moment? And can I lie to myself if I know about the lie? Can I fool myself or is the idea of wanting to be different the engine of change?

This search for answers, for easement. That there is information or knowledge that helps you immediately, that opens your eyes. But where could we find them? In the outside world or everyone for himself - in his deepest inside? As an example:

> The same mishap can happen to everyone,
> but everyone deals with it differently

The solution-oriented asks what he can learn from it. With the other it was bad fate again, with the optimist it will work the next time, the pessimist knew that this would happen. The irresponsible says that the others have failed and the responsible person blames himself. We can react to situations, but HOW we react is up to us - not the situation ...

What exactly is going on in our heads?

We are victims of our thoughts and feelings. We only consciously feel the effects and have to live with what works in us. But how far should we go with it? Are we really just victims of negative feelings and thoughts? Can we just watch the carousel of thought keep turning? Or can we also lead and decide? There is probably no small male or female sitting in your head and evaluates your life according to a "fun scale". Happiness and joy don't fly through the air. When you buy something great, the product doesn't give you an invisible helping of luck. Your feelings don't suddenly appear or come from anywhere. We have complex processes and interactions behind it:

Made up of trillions of cells and bacteria, up to 86 billion neurons in the head, which can make up to 1,000 interconnections. Your physical Constitution, the nutrient situation, your hormone balance, your memories, habits, the internalized way of thinking, your perception, the information that you take in, associations of thoughts, whether the sun is shining or how you slept. In addition, there are also your inner ratings, stress, problems, worries, needs, fears, joys and much more. Even the smallest thought you have, is like a drop in the Ocean of consciousness.

Nothing just arises in your emotional world. There are always processes and modes of action behind it. The processes always work neutrally. Processes don't care whether they create serenity or stress. Whether you're happy or sad doesn't matter for biological processes. The processes don't judge; they just work.

So what happened to us that we are so dissatisfied with so much? That we wear so many burdens? Because, in itself, we are just a highly complex organism consisting of cells and bacteria that is afraid of what could happen tomorrow. But where do these fears come from? Why can't we look at our life with serenity and confidence?

The pursuit of happiness

Happiness is an important part of our lives. We want it in love, in free time, at work, everywhere. I have never seen anyone who specifically wanted to be unhappy. There are people who do the craziest things just to experience happiness. Even religions or beliefs promise happiness - in this life or in the next. So there must be something special in our feeling of happiness, because other states of feeling are not so essential. Whether you feel brave or not, relaxed or not would be nice, but it is not as important as happiness. If you feel unhappy in one or more areas, it is quite a big burden. It's also very difficult for us to deal with. We try to distract ourselves so that we don't notice how unhappy we are. It really hurts. But why?

Of course, our genes are at the very beginning. They provide a certain framework and scope: how the body should develop? Which cells grow where and how? Which organs or functions are pronounced and how strongly? They can increase tendencies or increase probabilities. But the genes can also change in the course of life. Some genes can adapt to the circumstances so that the next generation benefits from this adaptation. The basic structure is mainly genetically determined. Pen and pad are the way they are. But which picture you paint with it is up to you - at least a little bit.

Below we have our instincts. They are the operating system, the programs, the basic behaviors that affect your feelings every day. The effects are always there, always noticeable: we have our sex drive (which varies depending on the hormonal balance during pregnancy). Our fighting or flight behavior or our survival instinct, which ensures that we stay alive and protect it. But first I have to want to live and this thought came to a French philosopher. He asked:

"Why don't we kill ourselves?"

This is a difficult but fundamental question. Why are we attached to life and what maintains the desire to stay alive? I have to want to stay alive and then I can protect it. There must be something deep inside that keeps us from wanting to take our lives. But it cannot be the fear of death. This fear can only work because we already want to live. Because the one who doesn't want to live anymore has fewer problems with death.

So we need something worth living, the desire to stay alive. If we didn't have that, it would be difficult for us to want to live. That's why we need a quality of life so that we don't want to take our own lives. But how does that happen? That we can experience nice feelings? That we can love, laugh and share? Because nice feelings feel good? Because we can experience?

Because we can experience satisfaction! Because everything just mentioned triggers satisfaction because it makes you happy.

We can do it all - and it all feels good too. And because it feels so good and only work for a short time, we want it again and again (like a drug addict whose "drug" is experience). We strive for happiness because it is an important part of our desire for life. We want to live because it feels nice - and if we don't feel it anymore, we tend to suicide (like a severe depression: satisfaction cannot be experienced, the dependence on life decreases and the risk to suicide increases).

In this sense, happiness and joy are not a simple "nice to have" - it is an (over) vital point. We want to be happy. We pursuit for happiness and we must also experience happiness. Without satisfaction, without the beautiful feelings that we could experience, there would be no value in life. Experience makes life precious. And those who experience nothing more actively or who can no longer experience beautiful emotions (like depressed people) literally get tired of life.

So what makes you happy?

First of all, it is the things that largely stand for a happy and beautiful life. Such as: health, a strong social environment, enjoyment, financial opportunities, physical activities such as sports, but also relaxation, good quality sleep, success, activities, fun at work and in leisure time. Time for yourself, time with others - and everything that feels good somewhere.

We all know these parameters and are (sometimes more and sometimes less) interested in complying with them. But the brain also has to play along: If I rate myself as too fat, then I feel bad after eating. If I don't have a social environment or have developed a certain dislike for people through bad interpersonal experiences, then I don't feel comfortable with people.

For example, I can treat myself to beautiful things and experience happiness, or I can consciously forego and experience happiness. But how could both be responsible for happiness if it is opposite? There has to be a different background, because otherwise "giving yourself something" would make you happy and "doing without" would make you unhappy - but it doesn't; both can satisfy you. Ask yourself:

How happy would you rate your life? On a scale from 0 to 10? How happy are you?

In itself, we are fine and if we think about it, we should also be happy, but it doesn't feel that way - especially not in everyday life. Although we have an enormous luxury that a large part of the world's population does not have, we quite often feel dissatisfied. We don't have to ask ourselves whether we get something to eat, we think about what we eat. Our existence is assured, our prosperity cannot be taken for granted. But how beautiful our life (overall) may be, we are rarely aware of it. In everyday life we quickly forget our luck and get angry about small things.

Maybe our happiness is not in the situations themselves? Depending on the point of view, we can paint the world colorfully and beautifully or drown in suffering. So what is the essential fact that decides our happiness? To answer this question, we would have to take a closer look at the various influencing factors inside:

It's about the associations, the habits, the internalized ways of thinking and behaving. Not what's on the surface. We have to look for your deepest processes and desires that are hidden. For example, how things are perceived and interpreted and how the brain processes this information. At the very beginning is the gateway between you and your reality - your perception.

PERCEPTION

I n the beginning was the light ... what falls on your retina, which converts it into electrical nerve impulses and creates an image in the brain.

* * *

We believe that everything we perceive, see, experience or feel comes from reality. This reality is omnipresent and we live in this "space" of life. We perceive it neutrally and interact with it. Our interaction is based on what we perceive. There is only one catch:

Our perception of reality

Because it is not what it seems. Our perception CANNOT show reality as we may think. Our picture of reality is so far removed from real reality that we couldn't even have a concrete idea of what real reality might look like. We can only say one thing for sure:

We perceive a fraction of reality because we can only see a small spectrum of electromagnetic radiation (visible light). By the way: woman have a higher density of color receptors, which allows them to perceive finer color differences. In general, we cannot see infrared, UV, microwave or X-rays. However, they are also present. We have no idea of reality because we cannot fully perceive it.

Our frame rate also influences us further. For our normal visual impression we have about 20 frames per second. That is our fluid picture of reality. A fly sees about 200 frames per second, which means that (compared to us) the fly sees in slow motion. If we were to transfer this high frame rate to ourselves, we would probably have had a different sense of time.

Our eyes (like all other senses of perception) are just receiver. They only receive the information and send it to the brain. Put simply, everything we see ends up on the retina (vice versa and upside down). But the retina is only the "collection point" of visual impressions. These informations are converted into electrical nerve impulses and transmitted to the visual center in the brain. There we have the primary and the secondary cerebral cortex field, which together produce a perceptible impression.

The reality is there, but because the brain evaluates the information, the force is not in reality but in the brain. This limits our picture of reality enormously, since we can only perceive what can be processed. The brain sees, hears, tastes, feels, interprets and acts. So we have an individual self-interpretation of reality - and that starts with seeing: Although we constantly blinking and the area of sharp vision is only as big as a fingernail (generously sized), we still see a lot. This is because we jump with our eyes about 3-5 times a second (without us noticing).

Or when we move our heads, we jump back and forth with our eyes so quickly that we can hardly see anything in between. We only see the beginning and the end. This does not blur our picture when we move our eyes. And even if we blink unconsciously - so we can't see anything - we still see. How does it work?

With a lot of imagination

Our fluid overall picture is an illusion and practically impossible. But this is not noticeable because the "picture interruptions" are not noticed. The moments when we don't see anything are simply overplayed by the brain. This happens with every eye movement, with every blink.

There are also "disorders" that affect the transmission of perceptual stimuli. Then optical stimuli are not transmitted regularly. However, the person does not notice this either because the memory takes over the image. This can be observed for example in traffic accidents. The people who caused the accident simply overlooked other road users because they did not appear in their picture of reality. No matter if pedestrian, motorcycle, car or truck. Everything can be overlooked. But what do we see at all?

Our visual senses never grasp an overall perspective, but are always focused: our nose is always in the same place. But we only see the nose if we pay attention to it. Otherwise it will not be noticed. But if you don't notice something, it doesn't work in the eye - it works in your brain. Only there can the information be classified according to its importance such as conspicuousness, movements, interests or focus. And the results of this classification are only perceptible to us in short-term memory.

Even if we have noticed something, it does not mean that we become aware of it. Everything that does not end up in short-term memory has not happened to us. This way we can again overlook cars etc., even though the visual stimuli have been transmitted (inattention blindness). There were also exciting experiments. The most famous experiment is probably the one with the man in the monkey costume: While people in a movie were supposed to pay attention to a special task, a man in a monkey costume ran through the picture several times. But a lot of people just overlooked it because it wasn't transferred to short-term memory. They have focused on their task so that other information has simply been ignored by the brain. The conspicuousness, our interests and our focus decide first what ends up in the short-term memory - the rest of the information disappears (like the nose or the monkey).

Our conscious perception is like a little flashlight in the dark. We cannot even consciously perceive a fraction of the total impressions that affect us. Some even suspect that the brain has to process around 11 million pieces of information per second. Because that would simply be too much, only the strongest information stimuli are consciously perceived.

We only feel it when the shoe presses. This is also quite good, because imagine that you are aware of all 11 million pieces of information per second. That would be too much. Unfortunately, it also has a downside. Because we only perceive in a focused manner, the problem lies in focusing. That, what is important to us at the moment has an impact on our perception. It works associatively, it is linked. What we see not only ends up in the brain and creates an image, it is compared and mixed with our entire knowledge. Here we find the fields of the cerebral cortex.

Reality meets fantasy

In the primary area of the cerebral cortex we have the picture of the outside world - the reality. The secondary cerebral cortex field (also called association area) creates a connection between reality and memories. The image of the outside world evokes a similar image from memory and only the result of reality and associative memory creates what we consciously perceive.

It seems that we always see the outside world neutrally; like a camera. But this appearance is deceptive. We don't see reality! We see always a mixture of reality and memories. (Recent studies even assume that our visual impression consists to a greater extent of memories than through optical stimuli from the outside world.) If we then blink or move our eyes, we only see memories based on the last impression.

Our perception has a lot more to do with our memories than we might think. Therefore we can react very complex and quickly. We use stored information material to interpret a situation, which is also very useful in dangerous situations.

So we could e.g. distinguish a tiger from a cuddly kitten. We saved both pictures and it was linked to the respective knowledge. The tiger was saved as a danger - and as soon as we saw it again, the respective knowledge (for the picture) was called up associatively; we were able to interpret the situation quickly and the body could react accordingly.

Through these learned connections we could and can recognize things (and also dangers) at all - and without much loss of time. We can't brainstorm for half an hour if we're in immediate danger.

Every song, every environment, every person or situation that we perceive always calls for the knowledge (experience and emotion) that we have saved. This enables us to recognize people, places or things in the first place. (If the secondary cerebral cortex field is damaged, the complete balance of memory and reality is missing and everything you see can no longer be recognized.) Any interpretation, evaluation, recognition or understanding is influenced by this process.

Conclusion

All of this together means that we can only perceive a fraction of the reality and everything we see then generates corresponding information that influences our evaluation. Basically, we NEVER evaluate reality. We always evaluate the mix of reality and stored information. In addition, all "unimportant" information disappears and everything that is important to us (right now) has priority. What all this means for us will come later, because the information that mixes with the perception stimulus is also an important influencing factor. Because we can primarily only refer to what we have stored as information - and that is what we call memories.

MEMORIES

Our memories are an important part of our being. Almost all of the experiences we have made are available to us. We can remember the most beautiful experiences and almost feel like we are experiencing them again. Our memories are not just "stored experiences". Our whole being is an expression of stored information. Some estimates go so far that we can store about 10 to the power of 150 information units. This is a 10 with 150 zeros. Our mental capacity (as a number: Quinvigintillionen) is beyond imagination.

But what exactly is stored there? Are they facts or is there more? And how strong is the influence of our memories on our daily thinking and acting?

How does it work?

At the very beginning, of course, is the storage process as such. In pedagogy there is the nice clarification of the meadow. The more often we run back and forth on a meadow, the more we trample down the meadow and then we can walk this path better. If we don't use this path for a long time, it will overgrow. It's the same with our memories. The more I repeat information, the better I can remember it. If I don't repeat it for a long time, I can forget it. This is our normal learning process. Like with vocabulary, rules, work structures or whatever. But it's not just our repetition, our feelings also have an impact.

Feelings are like a cocktail of information and also a part of stored information. If experiences have a strong emotion (positive or negative), then they "burn in". Then it's like a fire that burns the grass away, so there's no need to repeat it. For example, if we perceive the tiger again, we see the shape and size, then our brain checks what information it has stored (including the emotions) and we can react faster. The respective hormones are released, the emotions intensify and we act accordingly. If we survive, this experience will also be saved - in the category: tiger. The emotional highlights of the experience and the end of the situation are stored most. Did we survive? Have we lost a leg? Was our strategy successful or was it pretty close?

All of this is reflected in the highlights and the outcome of the situation. These are the basic structures of every stored situation. What is between the highlights is also saved, but not with this intensity. As a result, the "intermediate experiences" are forgotten more quickly and the imagination fills the gaps that have arisen.

So we have the repetition and the emotions. Both ensure how well something is saved. The better something is stored, the easier we can remember it. This process called "ease of recall" and gets better with every repetition. This means that the more information is repeated, the easier it is for us to remember it again. With countless repetitions, the path can even turn into a freeway - a neural freeway, which enables us to react at lightning speed. This is less about vocabulary of a foreign language; our complete being is an expression of it. (I'll go into this in more detail later.)

The process of storage and the pitfalls

In addition, in the process of saving (primarily) only your own actions, ways of thinking and behaving are saved. There is little capacity for others - especially we cannot look into other people's heads. We only experience our own thoughts, fears or worries, but not those of other people. Take yourself as an example: From everything you think, where doubts, worries or fears plague you, what comes out of it? What can others notice? What do we tell and where do we act accordingly?

It is like the tip of the iceberg. We (and everyone else) present only a fraction of everything that lies dormant in us. We cannot remember everything, much less the behavior of other people, or even their innermost feelings and thoughts.

Our experiences that we save and the memories

that we can remember are always self-related. We can imagine more situations and examples of our own behavior because we simply have more information about ourselves. As a result, they are not as realistic as we think. They are "one-sided". So we automatically assume that we always do more than others just because we have more information about what we do.

But, we don't just overestimate our own performance. We overrate ourselves, no matter in which area - positive or negative. If we are very self-critical, then our own reviews, quirks and mistakes are overrated. Then we always rate ourselves worse than we actually are. It follows how easily we can remember the behavior. That influences our feelings and our actions. The easier we can remember our abilities, the more we are convinced that we have this characteristic (availability heuristic).

It is the same in our opinions and beliefs. When we get new information, we can think about whether it's logical for us. But we can only weigh it up based on information that has already been internalized. Objective knowledge does not simply appear in us so that we can better assess it. Where should it come from? We can only compare it with what we have stored in the head. New information is compared to old information.

In addition, the information is evaluated based on the "ease of recall". Only that is important for the brain; how easily we can remember information. Whether it is right or wrong is unimportant and can hardly be estimated by the brain. The brain doesn't know what's true. It derives the inner beliefs from a frequent repetition - and so it becomes a fact. So the easier we can remember, the more firmly we are convinced that it is true. But that also means that the accumulated truths and beliefs need not all be correct. As soon as they fit into our concept of thinking, sound right and have been repeated enough, they will come true for us.

But it's not just our truths or opinions. The range of your beliefs is broad. Everything you believe is affected: your excuses, your fears, worries, or your justifications. We just have to repeat it often enough and then it will come true for us. So the truth has nothing to do with facts, but with conclusive explanations and a strong repetition.

Memories and associations

For example: What can you collect when you think of cars: the basic principle, the function, the equipment, the design, the brand or certain regulations. Take a minute and try to find as many terms as possible. Now think about what you can't find of cars and what has nothing to do with it - without connection or association ... that's more difficult.

It is the same in conversations when we answer. The appropriate information that we have on the topic is called up automatically and associatively. Or if we (unconsciously) change the subject, there is always a "bridge connection", a link between the subjects. It can be a word, a feeling, a memory, it doesn't matter. Here, too, the association connects the topics.

Not only our perception works associatively, but also our memories, thoughts and feelings. Everything is connected. When you feel bad, you can easily remember situations where you also felt bad. If you are well, it is easier for you to remember good moments. It always works the same way. If we have fun on Saturday evening, the world can stay as it is. Monday morning the world looks very different again.

But, if we remember, the information is not simply retrieved and then returned to the "folder". Each recall changes the memory because the current emotional state is connected to the memory. On the one hand, we can process terrible experiences (or traumas) if we combine them with positive, powerful or neutral feelings. On the other hand, we can also go deeper and deeper into sadness when our general emotional state is often negative.

For example: If we often experience negative situations or often feel bad, we create a very quick "ease of recall" that makes remembering easier. So we create more negative ideas and rate them even worse. The emotional state automatically calls up similar memories. Then the comparison of reality and memories largely consists of negative feelings and our general perception deteriorates. This quickly gives the impression that our bad feelings were justified. Equivalent memories, associations and the changed perception confirm our self-confidence. Because of the worsened perception and one-sided memory, we don't notice it either because we have no comparison. We don't exist twice, where in the second version of ourselves: we evaluate differently and have different experiences, whereby we can compare our perception of reality.

We could only remember if we were happier or more relaxed in the past. But even if we were, it doesn't mean we notice it because our current awareness is always automatically projected onto our past experiences. Who can remember everyday worries, strains or desires 5, 10 or 20 years ago? We already have a problem with last week. Even yesterday will be difficult: what did you think yesterday at this time? This is rarely saved.

Your feelings also determine which memories are recalled associatively. The feelings make it easier to call up similar feelings; like a search engine looking for equivalent emotions. The emotional state is decisive for the type and quality of memories and ideas. Or let's take uncertainty. If I feel insecure, I can remember uncertain situations more easily. This gives me more examples of my insecurity that confirm me (in my impression). The more often I feel like this, the more information I have about it and the easier it is to remember it.

This makes it easier for us to remember unsafe situations over time - situations in which we have often been criticized or felt unsafe. (The criticism does not even have to come from other people.

Most criticism comes from ourselves anyway, when we are in our thoughts.) And because we often think about unsafe situations, this assessment is solidified (by the frequency) and we behave us accordingly.

That works e.g. even with certain people we meet. If I have had bad experiences with certain people, certain customers or the (unsatisfactory) boss, then these experiences will be recalled associatively as soon as we see these people again. In this way, a "specified" uncertainty can arise - due to storage and association - which only occurs when we are in contact with these people.

So it is not the "real" reality or our character that decides how confident, insecure or good we feel, but how easily we can remember the respective situations in which we acted accordingly, how often we call up these thoughts (how strong the neural highway is) - and what exactly we recall.

Because it works associatively, we always automatically get an equivalent impression of the current emotional state and only the result of this determines our behavior. On this basis we define our properties and our character.

One more thing is very important. Our normal everyday behavior hardly triggers intensive storage stimuli. However, if we experience situations in which we feel bad or experience a lot of stress, we experience more intense emotions that make it easier to save them. This generates more memories in which we feel bad, because the moments in which we feel good are simply not saved. It's nothing special, nothing notable. When we experience uncomfortable situations, we also have stronger emotions that favor the process of saving. This tends to save more uncomfortable situations that distort our self-assessment or our self-image.

The variety of one-sided memories

"What you see is all there is"
Daniel Kahneman

We are therefore not always the way we see ourselves - we are more extensive. But we hardly notice this diversity because our memories cannot show this wholeness. Basically, memories are nothing more than memorized situations that are reconstructed based on a few saved key points. Just as we remember learned knowledge, we also remember past situations. But that also means that we can distort or confuse facts, events or memories. The emotional highlights and the end of the situation are the basis that form the framework of the memory. Everything else simply builds on it and distorts the current emotional state. We cannot say whether a memory was really like this or maybe different. We don't notice this mistake at all because we create our own construction to which we refer - and then we think it is true.

Let's take white light as a more abstract illustration. All colors (light waves) that we can see are present in white light. If you now take a prism (or something with a prismatic effect, e.g. the back of a DVD), then we see the rainbow colors - the light is broken down into its "individual parts" - so made visible to us. If we now take a "one-sided" prism (in this case our memories), which only shows green light as an example, then the impression arises that the white light must mainly consist of green light. This impression is deceptive, however, because it only shines through this prism.

It's the same with us. We cannot say that we (or others) are so and so, but we only see fragments, from which we create an overall picture. We also cannot describe white light with just one color because we only see one color. We see ourselves in a certain light, but we still have all facets of human behavior in us. Sometimes we have honest moments, sometimes dishonest ones. Sometimes we are loving and attentive and sometimes a little less. Sometimes we are respectful and sometimes we are narrow-minded. Sometimes we are confident and sometimes we are unsure. Sometimes we are active and sometimes we feel listless or lazy.

Although we have everything in ourselves, we only remember the most common attributes, with a tendency to positive exaggeration: Who is not honest, loving and respectful? But what if we are stressed, frustrated or tired? How respectful are we in a hurry? How loving and attentive are we when we are annoyed? How honest are we if we make a mistake? How helpful is our advice when it is for other people and how "wise" are we when it comes to ourselves?

Conclusion

In summary, this means that our beliefs are also determined by the type of memories and thoughts that we can retrieve most easily. It doesn't matter whether memories correspond to reality. Because, firstly, we can only remember what we have actually saved and secondly, it is emotionally changed with every recall, which further removes us from reality.

And that's the exciting thing: we think that our memories are facts, that everything is as we think: we don't even notice all the misjudgments, misinterpretation and self-constructions that remove us from reality. We don't notice them because we have no comparison.

So there is a lot more slumber inside than we are aware of. Whether we can change that is also questionable. Of course, we can pay more attention to this, but we cannot completely free ourselves, because they are simply fundamental functions of our biology. We could at most accept that our feeling is more than just an external reaction. Our anger or frustration is nourished by memories, nourished by the "ease of recall".

So our sense of consciousness is much more "fantasy" than reality, but it plays a key role in our sense of reality. What that means is coming now.

IMAGINATIONS

Our thoughts are not just a commentator, they have a significant impact on everything. It is the interface between the inner and outer world. The mind tells the body what the external situation looks like so that we can react in reality.

Because only our thoughts - the ability to mentally construct situations and remember them - lead to a past and an idea of the future. And then we can refer to these thoughts and interpret them. We are in constant interaction with the outside world. We react to external influences, perceive the large amounts of information with our senses and evaluate them. The associations, expectations and experiences that give us an overall picture are then used for the evaluations.

For example, if you have one in about 50,000 thoughts a day, an electromagnetic pulse is generated. The type of impulse determines which messenger substances are released. These messenger substances are chemical liquids that consist of various hormones. The "happiness hormones" include "endogenous opiates" - the body's own opium, so to speak (which I will call "opium" in the following). Depending on how and where the messenger substances are produced and where they are transmitted, a feeling arises.

This is what the brain does in continuous operation. Processes are continuously coordinated and thoughts are created. It is like a colorful dance by a swarm of bees that keeps itself alive as a collective. Of the 50,000 everyday thoughts, about 20% relate to memories (which are always a mixture of fantasy and reality), but the rest are speculations. That means 80% of all thoughts and ideas are pure fantasy.

Most of the time, scenes are constructed or evaluations are carried out. These are sometimes situation-related, sometimes inspired by our experiences and sometimes purely arbitrary. They move past our inner eye like clouds, barely perceptible, but still present. If there is a tiger in front of us, we must of course react to the situation and do something that will ensure our survival. The catch is that we can create mental stressful situations at any time. The "danger" only has to be in our thoughts and still creates stress or discomfort - a little digression.

STRESS

If there is a danger, the brain immediately switches to "emergency operation". All energy is sent into the muscles and all other processes go into economy mode. The immune system shuts down as well as digestion and thinking processes. The heart beats faster and at the same time the body's own hormones and adrenaline are released, which give us energy. Everything that keeps us alive in the long term is reduced and everything that is crucial for short-term survival (in a fight or flight situation) is started up.

This guarantees a maximum of strength to efficiently get everything that the body has to offer. The best-known main player is our cortisol, which is often referred to as a stress hormone. Cortisol is just an activity hormone. Without cortisol we would not get up in the morning. It is an antagonist to melatonin, the sleep hormone. But in dangerous situations, a surplus is immediately produced so that we become more efficient and productive. But what is a danger anyway?

Some researchers assume that we only have two innate fears that indicate a danger. The fear of falls and loud noises: As baby monkeys, we had to cling to each other so that we didn't fall down and noise was the signal in an emergency. The rest had to be learned "with difficulty" or arose with the development of consciousness. The fear of insecurity (darkness, death, future) only became a problem with the progressive development of consciousness. After all, a baby knows nothing about death or future worries, problems, and needs. It also cannot perceive dangerous situations, let alone interpret them. It doesn't know if a tiger is peaceful or hungry. In evolution, early humans had a handful of survival fears: hostile tribes, storms, predators, or lack of food. It was al about the struggle for survival.

The interpretation of dangers

But what does our everyday life look like? How dangerous is it? How dangerous is the queue at the checkout? How life-threatening are misunderstandings? If you had to rate your everyday dangers on a scale from 0 to 10, what would you think? Mostly it's 0, maybe 1, but what is still actively life-threatening today?

Real life-threatening situations in which we would have to actively fight or flee have become extremely rare compared to before or in other parts of the world - at least in everyday life in our society. The body is safe, survival is guaranteed in some form.

Our current dangers are therefore not so much those that we see or actively threaten our lives, but above all dangers that result from evaluations, thoughts and interpretations. For example: How often do we have money worries or fear of the future and how often do we experience an immediate danger - perhaps in the form of a bailiff at the door? How often does someone hold a knife to our chest (which would be an immediate and real danger) and how often are we just afraid? How often are we exposed to real danger and how often do we feel insecure? We hardly experience life-threatening dangers, but how often do we experience stress in everyday life? Hence the second question:

What is your daily stress level from 0 to 10? In daily work maybe 5, sometimes 3 and sometimes 7 - maybe at the weekend 0 or 1.

But it has nothing to do with our everyday dangers that we don't experience! We experience more stress than there are real dangers. And that's the point: dangers and stress go hand in hand, but we rarely experience dangerous situations in everyday life. Of course there are always difficult moments, strong problems and strokes of fate in life, but I am concerned with the normal everyday stress, which is mainly based on psychological causes.

When we interpret a situation as a danger, the first thing that is triggered is stress, which is an excess of activity hormones that affect our fighting or flight behavior. The higher the stress level, the stronger the "program" of fighting or fleeing. This process takes only a few hundred milliseconds. Like when we oversleep and have to go to work. You look sluggish on your watch and suddenly you are wide awake. Or, if you just escaped an accident: how quickly your body is flooded with adrenaline. The unconscious reaction from us (and the body) is faster than any thought. Only then can we think how tight it was, but there are no complex thoughts in the situation itself.

We first interpret the situation and then we can act accordingly. First, we need to know if someone is a friend or an enemy, or if the situation is dangerous, and then we can act as needed. In order to be able to interpret correctly, the type of evaluation is checked for perception, experience and thoughts that are generated in fractions of a second.

Now comes the essential: What is classified as a danger depends on the situation, experience and assessment. And since the assessment methods are individual and limitless, there are also limitless and individual dangers. But this also means that it is not the real danger that decides, because there are hardly any, it is our imagination that triggers stress. For example:

We sit comfortably and without time pressure in the car, drive from A to B, the sun is shining and we are lost in thought. We don't really notice whether a traffic light is red or green. It is indifferent. The traffic light does not generate intense stimuli because it is not important. We glide through the traffic like in a trance.

But if we're too late and have to hurry up, then the stupid sun is dazzling, every traffic light is on red and there are only idiots on the street. We get more annoyed with every red light and it is always the same when we are in a hurry. As if we hadn't already guessed that something like this would happen.

Objectively, both situations are the same. Only our perception is different, which changes due to our focus. What is important to us at this moment changes the assessment of the outside world and associatively the stored information is retrieved that we have about the current situation. The body then reacts to it. We generate activity hormones (stress, adrenaline, etc.), which we cannot break down while sitting in the car. This influence of emotions further changes our perception, which in turn influences the associations and we become more and more annoyed. But the problem is not the circumstance or the situation because: what is the fact at this moment?

We have not come too late, because we are still at the red light. There is also no real danger that threatens life immediately and now. Nobody holds a gun to our head - we are safe in the car. At the moment everything is safe and well. The only thing we have is a negative idea of the future that triggers a negative association and perception that emotionally stresses us. They are "only" thoughts. Our imagination that we might be late triggers a negative assessment of the future - and this negative assessment of the future means that we feel stressed now. So our imagination works without time, no matter whether we think about the future or the past, but the feelings that result from it can always be felt in the now.

A red traffic light or a traffic jam can be classified as a great danger if we are in a hurry. Many things to do, with little time. Misunderstandings, communication problems or things you don't want to accept. Disappointments, uncertainty, fears for the future, problems, worries, unfulfilled desires and so on.

They can be all causes of stress - and mostly they are. This means that the imagination and the resulting evaluation are crucial for our stress.

In addition, your own sensation intensity and the processing of the stimuli also play a role. There are people who perceive less well and there are people who have more intense stimuli of perception. The more intense the perception stimuli, the more sensitive these people are (but "sensitive" only means: "the perception of different sensations").

The sensitive person has more intense stimuli of perception, whereby he also perceives more intensely. He has more information that needs to be processed. This also allows him to imagine more. He is more creative and that is exactly the point. A more intense feeling and a higher level of creativity are also not a bad thing - in fact, both are very powerful. It can destroy you or unlock the greatest potential. The only question is: what is in control?

The external circumstances, the fears and doubts or the independence with internal control and a clear focus?

For example, if you are sensitive and dominate fears and doubts, you can nourish them very well with your imagination - and through the stronger sensation, these stimuli are also perceived more intensely. This increases internal burden and (depending on thoughts and circumstances) creates an almost permanent dangerous situation that triggers stress.

It mainly takes place in the world of thought, but becomes real through the intensity of the sensation. The activity hormones are released effectively and the better feeling makes them more noticeable. This in turn reinforces the recall of similar memories, associative thoughts and emotions. It is a vicious cycle that can be triggered by "little things" in everyday life.

As I said, the thought that you can't do something in time is primarily just a thought about the future. Based on experience and knowledge, we estimate the approximate time we need for the activities. If this estimate is negative, there is a risk: stress arises and your body produces more activity hormones. The tangible result then becomes part of your reality, even though the cause was mental.

And so it is everywhere. For all things, situations, people or behaviors, it is always the negative or dangerous assessment of the situation that creates stress in a split second. It is more intense for some people and less so for others. From time to time we can deal with the stress because we are designed for it. However, if stress becomes a constant condition or occurs at a certain frequency, it becomes dangerous for the body and mind: the immune system weakens, the digestion no longer works properly, muscles / connective tissue (especially the back and jaw *) are tense more often, which leads to an undersupply of the muscles in the long term. Due to the faster heartbeat, the blood pressure rises, the hippocampus regresses, which makes it harder for us to think and relax. The brain craves faster energy (sugar / carbohydrates / fat), which can lead to one-sided overeating, and so on.

*(There is also a nice trick: Pay attention to your jaw. The jaw is the first address for stress. When the jaw tenses, so you compress your teeth, you are experiencing stress. There are many small everyday situations where you get a tiny increase in stress. If you pay attention, you will find out how and when your body reacts. With this signal you can reflect on your reaction and way of thinking and you will see how subtly everything works. You can also work actively with your jaw. If you loosen it, open it wide or move it back and forth, it always helps a bit to release this tension.)

Conclusion

The much greater danger is therefore no longer

the immediately life-threatening situation, but the effects of our "survival program", which we call stress. The way stress works has helped us millions of years to ensure our survival. In an environment where the struggle for survival was always there, stress was essential for survival. But today, when our survival is assured, this protection mechanism has become one of the greatest burdens. (It is fascinating to see how we developed.)

Finally, we have to assess a situation as a danger - and that triggers everything else. A situation cannot evaluate itself. A situation cannot transfer its evaluation to us. Back to imagination.

* * *

But not only our risk assessment plays an important role. It is our general way of evaluating: how we deal with situations mentally when we experience something. Pay attention, think for yourself: when are you completely (with your consciousness) in the situation and when are you in the situation, but your thoughts are everywhere? Basically, we do nothing other than be in our thoughts all day. There is a nice story from the Far East that goes something like this:

One student asked the master why, in all his activities, he is always so calm and happy. Then Master said: *"When I stand, I stand. When I go, I go. When I cook, I cook. When I eat, I eat and when*

I sleep then I sleep." The student replied: *"But I also do that."* The master replied: *"No! When you stand, you already think about leaving. When you leave, you already think about the goal. When you cook, you think about eating and when you eat or want to sleep, you think about everything else."*

And that's the same with us! When are we completely in the situation with our concentration and attention - without thinking about anything? For example, when we are in a conversation or something is explained to us, we are rarely 100% focused on the other person. We can't really listen because we only think of the following in the conversations: when it's boring, we digress and when it gets exciting, we think about what we could say next.

We only hear fragments of the other person and create an overall package from them. It's not really listening. We don't really understand either because we ignore nuances and minor details, but these are often crucial. Give it a try. In a conversation, pay close attention to the other person without digressing your thoughts or thinking about what you want to say next. Concentrate 100% on the other person.

But it is not only noticed in conversations. Every activity or interaction in the outside world is affected. When are we really in the situation with all our concentration? If we don't feel like working, we are not always at work. Most of the time this thought comes before work - so it's an idea. Or we are at work and want to finish work now. Then our imagined future is more beautiful than the current situation. Then we "dream" permanently of the better future and we struggle through the day. If it is just before the end of the day, you feel better because the idea of a better future is getting closer.

Or if we are worried about the future, this troubling moment has not yet occurred - we are just imagining it. If we are unhappy with our current situation, then we imagined it better than it actually is. If we complain about not having enough money, it is just the idea that we cannot buy what we would like to have. We dream of more opportunities that we cannot implement financially. If we are afraid of the future, nothing has happened yet. It's just speculation. Even if something annoys us, the annoying moment is over very quickly. But we are holding onto the situation in our heads and could be upset about it hours or days later.

And while we are thinking one or the other of these, we are sitting somewhere and none of this is reality at this moment. They're just ideas that have nothing to do with the actual situation, but still make us feel worse. Here is another nice story from the Far East:

2 monks were on the move and came to a river. There was a woman by the river who did not dare to cross the river and asked the monks if they could help her. One monk looked at her, picked her up, and carried her across the river.

The other monk couldn't believe it because they were not allowed to look at women, let alone touch them. On the other side of the river, the monk let the woman down and the two monks went on. After a while the other monk said angrily: *"How could you look at the woman and also touch it? We have made a pledge, that's not okay."* The monk answered: *"I left her at the river. You still carry the woman with you."*

Ask yourself: How often do we actually experience (at this moment) situations that are stressful, annoying or worrying and how often do we only think of any situations that stressed us? And we do that all day long. Every thought (*"I don't feel like it"*, *"That annoys me now!"*, *"Why me?"*, *"I prefer ..."* etc.) changes biochemistry.

Our consciousness is like a situation analysis system and if we constantly think that we don't feel like it, where should it come from? If we often think that everything is annoying, how could we be calm or happy? If we constantly complain, whine, criticize and imagine more beautiful situations (if we only had this or that which we don't have), then we also constantly rate our situation worse. How could anything be fun if we judge everything negatively? But since everything is connected, such thoughts change your associations. This calls up equivalent memories, the perception adapts and the body reacts with the corresponding hormones.

Disturbing things and their consequences of

stress are often only the result of the constant repetition of certain thoughts. This means that the situation or thing (in the long run) doesn't bother us because it is quickly over, but the mental bias, repetition and construction: that we imagine it again and again and maybe also think about what could have gone better. All of this makes us angrier, even though the situation is different again.

The power of pulse intensity

We have the mental process (electrical nerve impulse) that releases messenger substances. And these messenger substances that are released give us a feeling that we then refer to. It doesn't matter whether the process is based on an external circumstance or an internal mindset, because the nerve impulses that are strongest are always preferred - no matter where they come from.

For example, if we experience an emotionally stressful situation, we have a strong intensity, but we only have this intensity during the situation. If we get upset about it later, the impulses of the external circumstances are long gone. The situation was unique at that moment. We did it, the moment is over and in reality everything is fine again. But not yet on the mental level. There it still lives - and how long or intensively it lives, everyone decides for himself: how strongly we hold on to the experience, how often we repeat it and how (good or bad) the ratings are. The constant repetition annoys us more and more because we experience it mentally again and again.

Remember!

If you experienced a situation that annoys you later, what was the situation and how did you feel about it? In the situation we experience it very differently, maybe react differently than if we remember it later and then get upset. The more we remember the situation or tell other people, the more annoyed we get. (Shared suffering is double suffering.) The point of reference was real, but the cause is mental. This means that you can no longer be disturbed by reality because the impulses from the situation have long since disappeared. But the impulses that come from memory keep it going.

We then construct the wildest scenes with utopian consequences and get annoyed more and more. As if in a mental rage, we forget every fact, every objectivity and only see red. It will probably never happen - especially not to the extent that we imagine it, but we can't get out of it. We are caught in a scene that will never become a reality. Caught in angry thoughts.

It is always the strongest stimuli that stand out from the crowd - regardless of whether they happen in reality or "only" in your head. Since the strongest stimuli are always preferred, we feel good or bad depending on the intensity of the impulses - and this need not necessarily have to do with reality.

We can also sit in a social group and feel bad. Then the thoughts that make us in a bad mood are more intense than the external circumstances. We can relax in the bathtub or worry. We can enjoy a sunset or have doubts. The (external) situation is always a purely possible trigger. The external situation can serve as an incentive to think in a certain direction - and as soon as we do that, all further impulses come from the brain. The reality is then past, but it is present in the imagination. It is effective imagination. The stressful situation is no longer your reality. The only thing that's still real is your memories of it. You keep it in mind no matter what the current situation looks like.

Marc Aurel

On the other hand, there is an exciting phenomenon that is directed towards the future. It's the same mechanism. Instead of "anger about the past" it is the "anticipation for the future":

If we feel anticipation, nothing really happened except the idea that we could feel better in the future. Be it the upcoming vacation, the upcoming weekend, a planned activity, a long-awaited purchase, the end of work soon and so on. The closer the specific project gets, the happier we become. Nevertheless, it is pure fantasy, with the thought that we will soon feel better. And only this idea of a better situation makes us happy. In such a moment, however, the better situation is not important (because nothing has really happened yet), but it is important to have the idea in mind that the current situation will improve.

The feeling of improvement

Brain research has shown that we get our own opium through mental or real improvement. This means that the improvements are important for our well-being. It doesn't matter whether we just imagine them or experience them through a successful experience. The impulses remain the same. It doesn't matter whether I'm referring to reality and assessing the situation as an improvement or just imagining it and evaluating it as an improvement. I have to rate something as improvement and as soon as I do I feel happier.

Anticipation is known to be the most beautiful joy, but it only takes place in your imagination. In reality nothing has happened yet. We are still at the same moment, but we feel better when we are looking forward to it.

On the other hand, we can also be very disappointed if there was no hoped-for improvement. Then we are "theoretically" no better or worse than before. Nevertheless, we are worse, although the current reality has not changed. Only the thoughts are different.

Anticipation and disappointment are a good

example of how our thoughts affect feelings. Thoughts that either improve or worsen, but thoughts remain "only" thoughts. Why shouldn't other thoughts have an impact? That is practically impossible. The principle always works the same. The strongest stimulus, the most intense impulse can be felt; and this "perceptibility" (what we call "feeling") is only an effect. A result that arises from the intensity of the stimuli.

But a symptom, a result can never be the cause. A symptom only shows us the way to the cause. Feelings are therefore not bad or something that you have to fight. Feelings are just an expression of your memories, evaluations and your physical condition. They show us where we come from and where we could go. Although they are pathbreaking for our further intellectual and factual behavior, they are not set in stone.

Our feelings are anyway in a self-made construction and that's why we sometimes feel better and sometimes worse. There is no stability. There are also no drawers in the brain in which our characteristics of patience, courage or cheerfulness are kept. There are only "familiar" thought structures to which we react associatively. But we can also take care of our feelings. If we feel bad, we could search for the origin by asking which of our own ways of thinking and evaluating triggered the negative feelings. Perhaps they were reinforced by constant repetition of thoughts?

And it's easier said than done. You get into rotating thoughts and frustration very quickly. Annoyed, we shift the blame or are angry about things that don't suit us - and can sometimes be extremely annoying. But what angered you at that moment? Nothing except the thought of it. None of our annoying thoughts are real at this moment, but they make us angry.

Everyday improvements

So on the one hand we have our opiates that result from an improvement and on the other hand we have our activity hormones (in excess: stress / deterioration / dangers). The main focus is now on improvement. By making our thoughts dependent on what happens to us, we link our emotional state to the situations. If we judge the situation as bad, there is no opium and we feel bad. To understand how joy and dissatisfaction basically work, we need to look at how we generally deal with situations:

- If I am dissatisfied with my financial situation and in vain long for improvements (e.g. great financial wealth that does not come about), there is no opium.
- If I am dissatisfied with my professional situation (for which there could be countless reasons) and there is no improvement in sight ...
- If I revel in beautiful memories or if I dream of a beautiful future, there will be opium at that moment, but at the latest after the daydream, I will fall

to the ground again.

- If I have wishes / goals that I cannot achieve (which means there is no improvement), there is no opium.

- If my vitality is bad, there is no opium.

- If I don't have time to make private improvements, there will be no opium.

- If the improvements achieved are not enough for me, because I want more and more or don't appreciate them at all, there is no opium.

- Do I have no goals, no projects or no ideas what prom-ises improvement or could promise improvement ... how else should it happen?

- When I'm constantly worried about something, over whelmed, or often upset (I'm thinking about deterioration) ... no opium.

- If I experience a lot of stress without (maybe visible) success or improvement ...

- If I don't see my success and just focus on the negative side of life, there is no opium.

- If I do not value myself, which means that I believe that I am not successful through myself, but only through "luck" or with the help of other people, the opium is scarce and I become more dependent on other people.

And then there are also sayings like:

"Life is not measured by the number of breaths we take, but by the moments that take our breath away."

That sounds good at first and because our everyday

life seems so boring anyway, we also confirm it. It seems logical, but it creates fundamentally wrong expectations. Because we don't (only) live in special situations. We live every moment, every second, every breath is life.

But if we only reduce our attitude to life to rare situations, then everything else becomes worthless and then we no longer arrive, but only strive (for the rare situations where we are breathless). But how often do we have moments like this - especially in everyday life?

We have countless opportunities for our satisfaction - it always has to be unique and special - and due to the mass of options, many little things lose their value. And if there are bad working conditions on top of that and the world continues to deteriorate, it is deterioration across the board ... and there is no opium.

As a result, we feel worse and worse, we don't see the "true" values - and if we don't deal with ourselves, but let ourselves be exposed and distracted more and more to the media, it is clear that dissatisfaction is increasing. Then it is clear that it is difficult for us to endure quiet moments because it shows all the mental rubbish that we can ignore as long as we are distracted.

Of course I don't want to downplay everything now - we have enough problems in this world; But there is a lot in our hands in the area of our well-being. We decide how we rate it and how strongly it affects us emotionally. It is because of our ratings or that we always rate everything worse, because we compare ourselves with the gloss and glamor from all over the world and think that the external appearance is all that matters.

But where should the improvements come from? We have to create them ourselves. We are responsible for it - nobody else. We are responsible for our own improvements and thus for our own well-being.

And if I only live from work to work and from weekend to weekend, I may have my handful of improving situations, but these cannot compensate the mass of countless problems, annoying thoughts or stresses. Then we mostly react to the negative feelings, so to the symptoms and accuse the circumstances: *"This stupid red traffic light.", "This stupid traffic jam.", "This stressful work.", This stupid problem.", "This annoying person", "The stupid (missing) money."* - and so on.

But if I only see the problem and not the solution, how can I find a solution or improvement? That doesn't work. That means that I have to develop completely different thoughts so that I can get out of the problem. And we do that every day - just a little more subtle: Suppose you're hungry. What are you doing? You make yourself something to eat and then you eat. At the moment of hunger, the thought of the solution (making food) is an idea of the future, how you can solve your problem.

You think differently so you can get out of there. You don't think, *"Crap, I'm hungry now. Why is this happening to me all the time? It can't be. Now I have to sit on the sofa with an empty stomach again, that's stupid. Why aren't the others hungry? Always me! I don't know what else to do?"*

No! You make something to eat and then you eat. You don't direct your thoughts to the deterioration and you don't get angry, you concentrate on the solution how you can improve your situation. You could also complain that you are hungry and focus on the problem - but that won't fill you up - and everyone knows that.

But a small gearwheel works like a big gearwheel. Why should it be different if we have a bigger "problem" than hunger? The task remains the same: problem + action = solution. This means that we should free ourselves from the mind's bias and think about possibilities (preparing food) instead of staying in the problem (being hungry). So what's our problem?

PROBLEMS

*"Every problem that concerns you gives
you the opportunity to grow."*
Unknown

A problem (originally: "What was provided (for a solution)?" It is not just there to annoy us, it's an effect of a cause from which we can learn to do better (in the future). It is a situation where the outcome is still uncertain.

But we play a key role in our situations and when situations are mostly negatively evaluated, no matter how they really are, we also mostly feel bad. We think that we are regularly in negative situations, but we don't even notice that we have evaluated them in this way or generated them ourselves. We portray ourselves too quickly as a victim who couldn't change the situation and blame the outside world. And sometimes we may be innocent, but the important thing is not the problems that haunt us, but how we deal with them.

It doesn't matter how full or empty the glass is

If I think the glass is half full, I can imagine that I still have enough. If I think it's half empty, it can be emotionally stressful, because maybe a half full glass is in the neighboring green garden. Ultimately, it doesn't matter (for the water balance in the body) whether the glass is half empty or half full. It is also irrelevant to discuss or worry about it. The main thing is that we quench our thirst and the body gets enough water.

It doesn't matter how we rate it. It is more important that we get it resolved. Because the moment the problem arises, it is a fact for us. Then it is part of the current reality and it is up to us to find a solution (or at least to become active in that direction). Let's take 2 unemployed people. Mr. P. (-essimist) and Ms. O. (-ptimist).

None of them are trying to find a job. Mr. P. complains and complains, blames the labor market situation and believes he can't find anything anyway. For this reason, his applications are very sparse. Ms. O., on the other hand, enjoys the free time, soon trusts in a job and even sparingly applies "because everything will work".

Of course, Ms. O. (compared to Mr. P.) feels emotionally better, but neither works. Whether I take care of the solution depends less on how I rate it. It doesn't matter whether I do something or not while I'm pessimistic or optimistic and then complain or if I downplay it.

Both have advantages and disadvantages, and both miss the target because the primary concern is to solve a problem and not to evaluate it endlessly while remaining in the problem. Because the story becomes even more colorful when Mr. P. meets Ms. O. Ms. O. should recognize the seriousness of the situation and should not take everything lightly, while Mr. P. should think more positively and should not pull a face (especially not in the interviews). And while the two are arguing, the jobs (fairytale) go to those who have consistently taken care of it.

When we evaluate a situation (or problem), it doesn't matter to the problem how we evaluate it. It is much more important that we get the problem solved or at least minimize the negative effects. It's about the solution - how we deal with it, whether we are looking for possible solutions or not.

There are only 2 different thoughts that lead to either one or the other result: *"I can do it"* or *"I can't do it."* It is like left or right, like problem or solution. Whether I think now *"I can do it"* or *"I can't do it"* does not matter at all; the earth will keep spinning. But everything else is based on these two thought impulses. I can only choose one direction. Either left or right. Neither is possible; I cannot classify the situation as unsolvable with hope and trust. There is always only one way.

Why we often underestimate ourselves

Just because we may not have found a solution does not mean that we will never find a solution. With all the possibilities in life, we are more likely to find a solution than not to find one. But that's so thrilling again: If we are worried about problems, they are usually "bigger" than in reality. We tend to construct the (mental) concern so big that we then feel overwhelmed. Why don't we think the worries and problems "smaller" so that we could solve them more easily?

Especially in difficult moments in life we often forget how good we are, what we can do or what we have already "survived". We can deal with problems, keep a clear head or strive for a solution. But that must first come to mind. As long as we don't remember it, it is not in our consciousness either. Our commitment or focus is always there, but it must also be used. Not in quiet moments and not on weekends, but exactly in situations that challenge us. So why don't we come up with the idea of fully exploiting our potential when needed?

This is where everything else comes into play: the perception, our associations, our ratings and so on. If I assess the situation as insurmountable, I feel bad. I lose hope of a solution and don't know what else to do. The perception deteriorates, the worry apparatus runs at full speed. Associatively I can't think of anything positive anymore - and the memories get worse. I carry these bad memories into the future, which makes them seem even more difficult and makes me even more unhappy. Instead of self-confidence, stress and excessive demands grow. But they are "only" associations. It is a snowball that triggers an entire avalanche - regardless of whether it is a problem or a sense of achievement. The processes always work the same. Let's take problem solving for further illustration:

I have a problem and will solve it. Now there are two and a half options:

1. I can be happy and proud that I was able to solve it. The problem is now past and has been successfully completed. This positive result of the problem solution is saved.

2. I'm annoyed that I had a problem. I get upset because it was unfair, I was innocent and so on. So it remains in the memory as a stressful experience.

1/2. Or I don't reflect it and my head is somewhere else again.

And this is exactly how our fellow human beings will react: Either they are happy for me that I was able to solve the problem, or they are angry with me because I had the problem or because they don't like my solution. In half of the case, of course, it doesn't matter to other people because their heads are somewhere else.

If I now rate it negatively and get annoyed with the problem (although it has been solved), the "visible" result is negative. I don't see the solution because I'm still focused on the (past) problem and I'm upset about it. I see myself as a victim of this "injustice" and have no sense of achievement. It is similar when our heads are somewhere else again. Then we see the solution only to a limited extent and depending on where we are with our heads, we feel accordingly.

However, if we focused on the solution and were happy that we could successfully solve it, it would give us strength, courage and trust. I then know from experience that I can deal with problems. That naturally strengthens my self-esteem. But, by the way, there is also an exciting phenomenon with the principle of feedback:

The insecure people mostly ignore the positive reaction. But they overestimate the negative rejection and evaluation. The rejection and criticism confirm their feeling of insecurity, which reinforces this feeling. Praise is more often ignored and criticism is preferred. It is the other way around with "safe" people. They only hear their positive approval and ignore any criticism. We tend to accept the opinions of others if we have the same opinion, regardless of whether it is criticism or praise. In other words, we basically only hear what we want to hear.

Again, we have a fine example of the impact of the associations. Because we prefer to perceive only what is confirmed with our view, and it doesn't matter how good or bad I rate myself and my actions. As soon as it is confirmed by others in the same way, I automatically assume that it really is as I thought. Our inner assessment is confirmed from the outside, the "ease of recall" shows that we can remember it better and the associations produce similar thoughts.

This agreement of various factors leads us to the only conclusion that it really has to be the way we think. As a reminder: When we experience and save situations, the highlights and the last impression are best saved. And if it was a problem situation, the peak is usually negative. But the last impression, how we get out of the situation, how we finally evaluate it and then feel, gives the final color. That determines the quality of the memory. Whether it will be an experience that strengthens or burdens me. It's one situation, but there are several ways we can deal with it. This affects our memories - and that determines our future actions and thinking. So there is no right or wrong (seen this way). But what we choose (with all its consequences) will become our reality; positive, how negative.

The root of the bad mood

All this means that the (internalized) type of assessment is crucial for how experiences are processed. It does not matter to the process whether we experience an improvement or a burden. It just works and doesn't judge.

After all, it is not the result, the feedback from other people or the situation that decides how we feel, but how we ultimately evaluate it, how often we experience it and what feedback corresponds to our view. And this point is extremely important for our whole life - our entire self-image, whether good or bad, is determined by this:

What success do I have?
- How do I rate this?
- Which feedback do I accept or which feedback is in line with my view?

What neural highways do I have?
- How many times have I experienced or thought about this experience?
- What kind of thoughts and evaluations dominate in my mind?

Therefore, our internal structure, how we evaluate it - and what results become visible is much more important. Ultimately, this determines what feelings arise and how we deal with future situations. Because of this complexity, it is sometimes very difficult to find the source - especially when we don't feel so good. So we can ask where our bad mood comes from:

*"Was it really (as negative) as I perceived it
or did my impression mainly result from my*

association, evaluation and interpretation?"

Now when we start asking where our bad mood comes from, it becomes very interesting. Don't just say, *"I'm in a bad mood, I don't know why"* or *"It's the person's fault"*, but just go ahead and search. There is always an inner trigger, a reason. It is an impact from a cause. It is not about the "question of guilt", but about the internal processes. So once again:

"What was the trigger for the brain to produce a bad mood?"

- Did we rate anything negative? Also in the form of listlessness?
- Did we have a negative experience that we often repeat mentally?
- Did our expectations not correspond to reality?
- Have we been disappointed and what inner conviction led to the deception?
- Did our perception play a trick on us?
- Have we reacted to a physical impact (thirst, hunger, lit-tle sleep, stress etc.)?
- Are we afraid of negative effects and results?
- Did we react (blindly) to an impulse?
- Have we taken it over from other people through perception and associations?

In this way we can understand it better, find the real cause and free ourselves from it. For example, if I notice that in a negative situation I have doubts -

and the situation is improving - and the doubts continue, the doubts must have a different origin. The external situation may have changed, but not the internal one.

The same applies to larger problems. When they are resolved and minor problems arise at some point, they are often equally stressful. Then it helps to remember the bigger challenge. The loads are almost the same, but the problems were different. So I can say that it was not so much about the different problems, but about my way of evaluating.

Remember that everyone has experienced situations in which they have been subjected to severe stress. Situations that were very stressful and that we "survived". Maybe they were a few years ago, but it doesn't matter. When a new situation arises that takes us out of everyday life, it helps to remember the bigger challenge from the past. We have mastered bigger challenges and why should we burden ourselves equally when there is a minor problem?

But it's not just about doubts or problems. Even if you just feel strange, shaken, or somehow think everything is stressful, it can be very fascinating if we look at the roots. Sometimes there doesn't seem to be a real trigger to explain this. In most cases, they are neural highways.

And when we become aware of it, it "clicks" and we realize that there was nothing to realize. We notice that it was unfounded, that it was a desperate attempt to hold onto the past. We are only used to doubting or complaining, so we automatically look for the problems in the situation - and that is very natural. In the past, people always had to be on guard. A possible danger could be hidden everywhere and in order to recognize this in good time, potential dangers were played through mentally. We have always looked for the danger, the catch in the situation - especially when we are stressed.

And since everything always has two sides, with advantages and disadvantages, we always find the good or bad in the situation - and that's the most exciting thing. It doesn't matter whether it's doubts, annoying problems or stressed feelings. If you find out for yourself how you got upset about big problems, how you doubted in uncertain moments and now, despite better circumstances, are still upset or in doubt, how could it come from the circumstances? That is practically impossible. The only thing that has remained constant is you with your mind. Like I said:

A special situation that happens to us is largely the result of our previous ways of thinking and acting. Then we experience this situation and if we don't like the results, we blame the situation and feel bad. But a result cannot be guilty. At best, the cause can be responsible (our actions or our omissions), but the result is innocent. I can't be angry with a result just because I don't like it.

Home-made simply tastes better

However, if we only pay attention to the result and

ignore our involvement in the "history", we over-look the causes, find no solutions and cannot learn anything. Furthermore, we can be infinitely upset and transfer all feelings of guilt and frustration to the situation or to the person. So our carousel of thoughts is strengthened by feelings of guilt and we have again created a new castle of dissatisfaction. But:

What will remain of it in 1, 2 or 5 years?

When we have a problem, we often think in final-ities. We only see the problem and our future ends with it. As with a small doomsday, all of our think-ing revolves around this one problematic scene - frozen in time. But if we think further (in the sense of time), then we suddenly realize how the world - and our everyday life - will continue to exist. We will survive it. The problem will end up in the bucket of time - sooner or later.

Even if there are only small "problems" that annoy or excite you in everyday life, you can ask yourself what remains of it in 2 hours, 2 days or 2 months ... mostly nothing remains, except perhaps a valuable life experience. And we can also use that for ourselves. If something happens that strains our nerves, we can say to ourselves:

"Now I have no time or desire to get upset about it. I'll do that tonight at 7:00 p.m. Then I take 10 minutes for it."

If we make an appointment for our anger, the frustration usually fades over time and we feel better again. It's like food that needs to be digested before new food can be eaten. If nothing is digested any more meals would be inconceivable.

And we would also have to digest our (possibly negative) situations, extract important nutrients (knowledge, life experience, etc.) and let go of the rest. Because there will always be (with every meal and with every problem) remnants and superfluous things that no longer have any sense or use for us. We can no longer get anything important from it. Then it just has to get out to make room for something new. Getting angry, holding on to it and judging it or whatever doesn't help you and only increases frustration.

And if you are really angry where no thought impulse helps, just bite a pen lengthways. This stimulates the same muscles that are stimulated when you laugh and the brain responds accordingly. After 2 minutes you have built up such a strong muscle stimulus that your brain can do nothing more than feel better. Try it. If you only bite the pen for a few seconds, it has no effect because the intensity is lacking. But if you manage 2 minutes, it doesn't matter how bad you felt before, afterwards you actually feel happier. (Only the most dominant impulse decides.)

And that has nothing to do with oppression or anything. When something stupid happens, we're not in a bad mood forever. At some point we feel better and with the pen we can speed up the process. Instead of the impulses of the bad mood slowly fading, we generate new impulses of the good mood. In this way we can turn "sometime" into "now".

But it doesn't even need a pen. We could also pay attention to the corners of our mouth in everyday life and pull them up a bit. This slight tension in the corners of the mouth not only makes us feel better, but also makes us look friendlier. (In addition, it is always interesting to observe when we pull the corners of our mouth up slightly; where we think, where the corners of our mouth should be and where they actually are. Give it a try too. Look in the mirror. It is fascinating what small "posture" on the face can make the difference.)

You are your guideline

In addition, the question may arise, how true is it to change our feelings? But what is real? Especially in the area of our consciousness or our feelings? Nothing is real there. They are permanently generated by our biology. We are not body and mind either, we are a "body-mind" so to speak; it is connected. Every sip of coffee, every painkiller or alcohol influences. Sports, relaxation or activities as well. Our consciousness, memories and thoughts work in constant interaction. With every idea, action, interaction or intake of food, we change our biology and thus our sense of consciousness.

There is also no golden thread in our sensation

from which we could deviate. Above all, a "golden thread" would mean that our sensations would be predetermined - and if they were predetermined (by whatever), how could free will work? The hormones and impulses, the bacteria and cells, the messenger substances that arise from the thought impulses, with their effect and networking, generate our feeling of life - every moment anew.

And by the way: What do "actually" bring us stressful thoughts (frustration, anger or reproaches) when they often have no influence on our everyday behavior? We have to keep going. We don't let ourselves be influenced - only in our mood and feelings. These are then on the ground until they have recovered. We simply endure the problem or live out these negative feelings to the fullest, but continue to act as before. So why the whole thing?

But there will probably always be a certain level of emotion that could strain us (in stressful moments). The only question would be, what dominates in your everyday life? Is it joy or suffering - and what are their advantages or disadvantages?

As examples: Fearing that I might forget my experiences and knowledge, I only started writing. Because of my stubbornness, I worked more and harder, which made me very successful. We stay calm for fear of rejection. We are more committed because we fear that we might lose our reputation or because we want recognition. Because some people have had a lot of bad (or even terrible) experiences, they have taken refuge in their own worlds and written the greatest books or invented the greatest things.

We can draw a lot of strength and perseverance from the fear of not being good enough. We can sometimes draw so much energy from anger or disappointment that we can exhaust ourselves extremely (through useful activities - cleaning up, exercising, etc.). Out of strong personal dissatisfaction or self-doubt, the foundations can be created to significantly improve life - and only because of the dissatisfaction can so much energy arise that we can really change our lives.

And it's the other way around too. If we have too much patience, our desires become a gamble of circumstances. If we are too helpful, we can become very unhappy because we keep putting ourselves back. If we are too optimistic, we can underestimate dangers and risks. If we see ourselves as too special, we will be pretty lonely at some point.

In theory, we can condemn everything and idolize everything. Every positive quality could be crushed in the air and every negative quality has advantages. There are always enough advantages and disadvantages for everything. Even in friendliness and helpfulness one could interpret selfishness or the suppression of one's own dissatisfaction.

Therefore, the evaluation of the characteristics is limitless, individual and almost meaningless, because (depending on the type of evaluation) each characteristic can be interpreted well and badly. It is not the fact that decides, but the information that is used for the evaluation. It is a matter of opinion. However, one consideration could serve as a guideline that somewhat simplifies this fact:

"Is my fear, doubt, worry, uncertainty, impatience, dissatisfaction or my sensitivity an engine or a brake?"

Good can be bad and bad can be good. Of course, depending on the situation, circumstances and degree of stress. We cannot badly describe everything about negative qualities, nor can we idolize the positive qualities. Therefore, we cannot say exactly what is good or bad. What can be bad at times can turn out to be good or great in the long run. What may look like little success in the short term can bring great success in the long term. What we define as poor quality in terms of our behavior can also turn out to be useful quality in another area. So there are many ways to get from A to B. Doubt or fear can be as motivating as joy or passion.

Conclusion

It doesn't matter what the situations look like. The brain interprets, evaluates and creates something that we can feel. We can blindly follow these feelings (and get upset when something stupid has happened) or look for the inner causes. Not so that we suppress something, but to understand that our feelings are only an effect.

Finally our brains can do everything - there are

no limits. We can criticize everything or find everything good. We can imagine the world colorful and
beautiful or drown in suffering. Everything is there:
From the unbearable cruelty to the miracle of life.
Everything is present in the world and everyone decides for himself which part of it becomes reality.

And it doesn't even have to be the big suffering or
wonder of the world. It is mainly the little things
that take place in your everyday life. We can forgive
other people or we can get upset. We can show our
pride or apologize. We can doubt or trust. We can
interpret everything into everything. Back to the
Imaginations.

* * *

But, again, they are "only" thoughts. Everything
we think determines everything else. It's about
everyday evaluations: of yourself, your everyday /
life, your interpersonal experiences. Every thought
matters. Every thought (like the snowball) can trigger an avalanche. And the nature and quality of
these thoughts has an impact on all other levels.

Feel your thoughts

Our thoughts are mostly unreal; they refer to the
past or are simply pure fantasy. We can always think
of everything, regardless of space and time. We can
imagine situations that actually took place, but
other people's reactions or the interplay of differ-

ent situations consist of so many influencing factors that we can hardly mentally consider them. It is far too extensive. Above all, our thoughts are every-where except in the current reality. Do the test. Watch yourself and your thoughts. Ask yourself:

"What is real now?"

And I mean this question seriously. As I said, how often are we with our thoughts in the current real-ity? Does what you think really have anything to do with current reality? Are there any thoughts that will help you develop constructively? Or are they just a few scenes from memory?

We have the impression that our thoughts depend on reality, but they are controlled by our emotional state.

Your emotional state and your memories deter-mine the course of your imagination. It is not the fact that nourishes our thoughts, but the feelings. This limits our thoughts about reality enormously, since we can hardly take into account the object-ive situation (in the imagination). It works associa-tively and equally. For example, when we are upset, emotions guide further thoughts. But since it works associatively, future thoughts correspond to the same emotionality. This means that the emotions are the basis for further ideas: a different perspec-tive, an emotional distance or a neutral assessment of the situation is difficult because they consist of different emotions.

Only when we have "calmed down" do we have a different emotional state and can then think about it more neutrally. So we can call up other memories (with different emotions) that give us a different picture. There is always only one way: So I can't feel bad as long as I'm happy. I can't feel brave when I think in fear. I can't think clearly when I'm stressed. None of this is possible because it is connected. If it were independent, I could **feel** brave and **think** in fear at the same time - but I can't. I may be able to overcome my fears and act, but I don't feel brave yet. Thoughts have and generate feelings - and the feelings evoke associative feelings that influence other thoughts. It is an interconnected cycle.

(Fun fact on the edge: We, for whatever reason, assume that the world should be the way we want it to be. And as soon as something differs from our: *"This is how the world should be"* view, we don't feel well. Why is our opinion all too often the benchmark for world events? Most of the time we can't change anything anyway. We can only get upset that it is not as we had imagined. But the world is not made to be responsible for our personal happiness.)

We are busy thinking about our thoughts all day. We think that they reflect reality. But reality only serves as a basis; All other thoughts are associatively controlled by the memories and the emotional state.

The little success

Remember: happiness and joy don't fly through the air and choose their "victims". When I buy something, no invisible portion of happiness goes from the product to me. It is always the brain that interprets the situation and produces the respective feelings. The anticipation only works because the improvement now makes us feel better, because opiates are released.

The goal is always an improvement, regardless of whether it takes place in reality or just in thinking. But an improvement is nothing more than a sense of achievement. We need success and then we feel good too. It's not about great wealth or luxury, it's very subtle. Every harmonious coexistence, a good food or a praise mean an improvement for the organism, mean success. However, if we are denied praise, we feel worse. We couldn't improve anything. Now there are 2 options:

Either we wait for external influences to give us the chance to make an improvement or we take action and make improvements ourselves.

We could pay attention to the small success stories and improvements in everyday life. Every action or obligation that we (have to) do in everyday life is an improvement on the previous situation. Our entire everyday life is full of situations in which we solve minor problems and from this we can also make improvements.

In all areas of life in which we create, do or endure

(no matter how subtle or self-evident), it means a positive experience for us if we take a moment and realize that we have created success. Regardless of whether we have prepared a coffee or if we had to endure an annoying customer at work. It doesn't matter what we do, because every completed action is a success. We change the situation according to our wishes and desires - even if they are only small.

We have to do the necessary everyday things anyway and why not use them for our intellectual benefit? The commitment doesn't matter whether I'm in a good mood or a bad mood. The fact is, I have to do it. How we react and what we make of it (at the moment) influences our future - real as well as mental. This moment of decision is always there. Every second we could think:

"Success! Thank you for this unique experience."

Of course, it doesn't always seem to be easy to apply this energy and show gratitude. But it works because the processes work that way. We use a certain functionality of our biology. It is just a matter of your own priorities. We can still be calm and improve the situation or solve the problem - just because we don't get angry doesn't mean that we don't care.

Our desire to improve something is evolutionary. It is deep within us and all our actions and efforts (all of our progress) are an expression of it.

And we want it for us too. The goal is always improvement. We can give it to ourselves or wait for it to come from outside. We and our biology simply play a decisive role in reality - not only through our actions, but also through our thoughts and evaluations. This leads to our neural highways and then to our (automatic) actions and habits.

> *"Think about what to do. Forget what*
> *you've already done."*
> Marie von Ebner-Eschenbach

It doesn't matter whether you actively think about improvements or whether it takes over the internalized processes. If you make it aware on a regular basis, at some point it will also be internalized and work automatically. If we give ourselves success after every action, we can improve our everyday evaluations without spending a lot of time and experience more joy in everyday life - thanks to opiates.

But that's not all. Since everything is interrelated, this also affects other levels. The multitude of success stories also improves our self-confidence and our perception. We are more neutral about things. The opiates make us more relaxed, stress-resistant and the type and quality of associative memories improve because more positive experiences can now be accessed. This in turn affects future challenges that are less burdensome for us, and the clearer perspective means that we can find a solution faster.

Because, as I have said many times, mass is important to the brain and how easily I can remember the success. The mass of saved experiences is always used as a template for automatic actions - and the more examples I unconsciously call up, the more I am convinced and act accordingly. The amount of experience is critical to what we remember. The only thing we have to consider is that we act regularly. That we save every action as a sense of achievement by giving ourselves success.

It is also not about closing your eyes, suppressing problems or not accept them. And I am not concerned with estrangement from reality, but only with a certain degree of internal control so that we can remain clearer and act in a more targeted manner. When we are clearer and more goal-oriented, we no longer worry about problems, but ensure that they are solved. Especially when we start evaluating all the accomplishments and commitments in terms of success, that's not a bad thing. We only pay ourselves the respect we deserve. Our brain works that way anyway.

Regardless of whether you think about improvements or deteriorations; consciously or routinely, but it will continue to work that way. The functionality is there. It doesn't matter whether we wait for something big to happen, that we (automatically subconsciously) evaluate it as an improvement and then feel better, or whether we consciously create improvements and then feel better.

The mode of action remains unchanged. For the process and the world out there, it doesn't matter whether it's a coincidence (from outside) or yourself with your active consciousness. It could only be important for your emotional world.

Thinking is not acting

The hardest and most important thing about such "forms of thought" or "exercises" is real action. We do something, but what? We start pondering, doubting or fall into deep thoughts. But if we just think about it, we get the impression that we have already done something. But if we just think about it (without acting), nothing will change.

We can even generate enormous pressure if we constantly ask ourselves whether we are exactly as we imagined it: *"Am I happier, more confident or more relaxed at the moment?"* These questions are useless and are not the goal. You can even make everything worse - especially in everyday life. So we only focus on the results and no longer on what leads to the desired results. Then every situation is weighed and everything that does not make us completely happy is condemned.

Here the focus is crucial: if I want more self-confidence, but focus on my insecurities, it won't help. If I want to be more relaxed but just think about what is bothering me, the stress will increase. If we only focus on our feeling of satisfaction and constantly question our feelings, we will only become more dissatisfied.

If you just pay attention to how you feel, you cannot change anything. Leave the feelings as they are. Pay attention to the processes, the goal and what leads to the results. We would have to pay less attention that we pay attention or create pressure, in the sense of: *"I wanted (not) more ..."* or *"Why can't I ...?"*, But we should be: draw attention to the experience. Do it.

We should focus on what we want to do and then act. Don't think you want to think about improvements - really think in improvements. Don't complain about your situations, but really reflect your perception, associations and evaluations. Don't think that you can pay attention to the corners of your mouth, but also pull the corners of your mouth up slightly. To become active.

We would not have to implement it 100% dogmatically. This is difficult at the beginning. It is far too complex for that. But, the more often you think in terms of success, reflect on your thoughts or pay attention to your perception, the better your sense of it will be. Set yourself the goal as 80% - and if you get annoyed then just tell yourself: *"Okay, that was just my 20% frustration."* This way we can experience and enjoy the beautiful feelings much more easily; without inner pressure or coercion.

Only through active action can we achieve the desired change, which gives us internal control and so much more. The focus must be on the goal; we should just do it. Somewhere there may also be a desire to really want to change something. We have thoughts of a big change in life, but we hardly implement it. In everyday life, such thoughts quickly fade away and we leave everything as it is. I also think most people know that. We know what bothers us, what annoys us or what we want to change. We even know what we can do if we want to achieve something. We just have to do it. After an action, you always feel better. Each (successful) "survival" of a challenge always makes you happy, content and strengthens your psyche.

But why are we still so lazy and have to pull ourselves together more often than we would like? We know that it is good for us. Just as everyone knows what they have to do to be healthy: eat healthier and more varied. Everyone knows how he would get to know other people: going out and making contact with people. Everyone knows how to make loved ones happy, but we rarely do.

We know everything in quiet moments. If we think about our future actions, we can do anything. After work, we can play sports, eat healthy, act confidently and purposefully. But in the middle of it, after work, in a stressful situation, in the queue or in everyday life, things look different again.

As I said, we know so many things without making anything out of it or implementing the knowledge. It was found that external knowledge has little influence on our actions, as long as we have no (own) experience, no "eye-opening" experience or have not developed a routine. So I can know as much as I want - as long as it doesn't become an experience or a big "click" in the head, the knowledge of my behavior has no influence on me. In this sense, knowledge is useless even if we have no experience with it. We only get the (necessary) experience when we act.

Let's take ourselves as an example: What do you know (-it-all) and what do you do with it? When we compare all of our knowledge with our initiative, it's very scary. There is a big difference between what we can imagine and what we ultimately do. But why? Do we lack the experience we would need to implement the knowledge? Is it the lack of independence that we don't start to act? Are we lacking motivation or will? What exactly is it?

THE WAY OF WANTING

and what habits have to do with it

> *"If we just let ourselves drift in life, we shouldn't be surprised that we don't get anywhere."*

So that we can act, we need an impulse: we want something. Brain tests have shown that this mental impulse releases dopamine, adrenaline and cortisol (a whole hormone cocktail). For simplicity, I'll limit this to dopamine. So: want = dopamine = energy (for the action) = feelings of happiness / opiates after successful completion. (Depending on the effort, some morphine is added to relax afterwards, e.g. after a workout). That's how we work.

At the beginning there is always the mental impulse that we need for an action. When it comes to basic physical needs, the impulse comes naturally from the body, but this can also be determined by external influences. Sunlight, for example, determines how much cortisol and adrenaline should be released in the morning. We notice that e.g. in the dark season of winter. The lack of light means that less activity hormones are produced and we automatically feel more tired in the morning.

In addition, I always need the idea first and then I can implement it. I can't just implement something and have the idea afterwards. We always need the impulse beforehand. With an active action it is also very clear: I have the idea that I want to chop wood - and then I also chop the wood. I can't just chop wood and then come up with the idea. In the beginning there is always the impulse, the idea. It is not so obvious in our behavior, but our behavior or way of thinking are also actions. This means that my behavior, my reaction or my way of thinking is based on an earlier impulse - and depending on the type and quality of the impulse, we behave accordingly:

Ideas / impulses = actions = experiences = knowledge, beliefs and routines = (basis for future) ideas / impulses = actions - which in turn become experiences etc.

This functionality of action, storage and resulting experience, which in turn determines the following action, works for a lifetime. Always. For certain skills we call this "experience" - on the way there we call it "learning". In our daily thinking and acting we call it different: there we call it: "habits".

You are the inner couch potato

Strictly speaking, we have no habits at all: Activities and information that we repeat regularly develop strong neural highways - which we then call habits. It is a solidified action plan that tells us from stored experiences what and how we could do something. It is like a behavioral memory, in which all knowledge and ability is stored. (People who have lost a part of their body can still feel severe pain in the amputated limbs because the information is stored in the brain. The lost arm can no longer hurt, but the brain still has enough information to trigger certain sensations. (Phantom pain.))

But our habits are not only responsible for the sofa, they can do much more. Here I have to take a quick look at other processes:

Human biology is always about stimulus processing - the interplay of hormones and impulses. The various organs take care of the hormones and electrical impulses are transmitted via the nerve cells. (The intestine has over 100 million nerve cells, but the brain has almost 90 billion. In proportion, the intestine has "only" 0.11% "brain portion" - so it's not that much. Nevertheless, we can feel the emotions in the stomach: it can "turn around" or cause a joyful tingling like butterflies.)

If we lose patience, for example, there is a nice metaphor: the barrel has overflowed. But behind it hides an "over stimulus" in the frontal lobe. The people with patience has less intense stimuli in the frontal lobe, which means that they can take longer stimuli. People without patience are stimulated more intensely, so that they reach their limits more quickly.

The barrels are the same size, but the drops are different in size. We call the result of this process patience, but from that point of view it does not exist. There are only stimuli with different intensities.

Everyone has patience. Everyone has certain actions, routines or situations in which the stimulus intensity is not so strong - and can be patient accordingly. Here we can see the principle of saving again. If you think that you have no patience, then remember: Without intense stimulus there is no reason to save the situation. It's nothing special. Only when the frontal lobe "overflows" do you have a strong impulse to save this situation. This automatically creates more situations in memory in which impatience (and generally intense stimuli from negative experiences) dominate.

The general question now would be: what leads to intense stimuli?

First there is biology, what means a less well developed frontal lobe. The frontal lobe regresses in people with chronic stress, high alcohol consumption or certain diseases. Even with children, this is still in the development phase, so that less patience can be found in these groups.

Regular exercise or varied brain work strengthen the frontal lobe. For the sensitive people, for example, the stimuli are always stronger, but what matters is where the focus is and how all of this is evaluated. Because the situation with our assessment plays an important role together.

Are we focused or often distracted? Do we have joy or do we get angry? Do we focus on the other person, on the task or do we want to get out of the situation as quickly as possible? Is the body well or are we in pain? Do we rate the situation as safe or dangerous? (In the event of danger, stress is triggered, the frontal lobe is affected and this changes the intensity of the stimulus.)

As soon as something bothers us, the stimuli become very intense. When we are disturbed in our harmony, in our focus, in our task or in the implementation; by other people, by lack of understanding, noise or by a deviation from imagination and reality.

The internal assessment simply plays a big role. Our idea of the "perfect" world serves as a template and as soon as reality deviates, there is a conflict. Socks on the floor can therefore be just as "annoying" as a barking dog; although the socks cannot actively disturb.

It is not so much the situations that trigger the stress, but our internal assessment methods. The brain interprets the situation and, depending on the situation, we have learned to fight or to flee. We are just used to it and the mass of countless experiences gives us the voice that gets angry when something annoying happens: *"I can't believe that this has just happened"*. That shows us the conflict between expectation and reality.

But it's the same voice that tells us to brush our teeth. It is the same impulse that tells the marathon runner to hold out, that tells the musician what notes he will play next. Our experienced handling of actions at work or the impulse that we trigger stress when we are in a certain situation - it's the exact same voice that keeps us on the sofa. Every state of mind, every enjoyment, certain reactions or activities that we like to do; everything that defines you arises from the processes of strong repetition.

Or let's take driving, for example. Who is sitting behind the wheel? Your habits. Any automated activity where your conscious concentration is no longer required is an expression of your habits. A change in your habit is always a change in yourself.

We have given names to individual processes and effects, but there is a big deal behind it. Everything is connected and everything affects at all levels. Basically, we are our own habits, since everything has only one origin. You yourself are an expression of your inner sofa potato with all your wishes, expectations or fears - a result of your internalized information.

> *You cannot change your habits; you*
> *can only change yourself*

If you want to change a habit, you have to change

yourself. Then you would have to act differently in the same situation to get a different result. And changing your actions is often difficult in the beginning. Only through regular actions can new experiences arise that the brain can automatically call up in the future. As soon as the brain breaks new ground, a new neural highway will emerge - and this will serve as a template for future actions.

But, in the end, everyone can have fun with everything. As I said, there is no fixed "fun scale" in the brain in which a small man / woman sits and controls and evaluates the respective activities based on the diagram. There are only certain parameters that must be met in order for us to get our opium.

Pain or gain

Avoiding pain and gaining happiness is the top priority of the brain. The gain or improvement must always be more bearable than the pain or the effort. An internal balance sheet is drawn up, so to speak. From the memory / experience it is roughly estimated whether the feeling of pleasure outweighs the pain / the effort - if it is, it is fun, we are motivated and act accordingly. If it's negative, we have a problem getting active. We feel bad, upset or stressed. The energy gain (improvement, joy, satisfaction) must be worthwhile in comparison to the energy costs (stress, effort or pain). As a scale, we can make this very clear:

$$\text{well-being} \text{———————} \text{pain / efforts}$$
$$\text{(+ energy gain)} \qquad \wedge \qquad \text{(- energy costs)}$$

The general problem lies in activities and things that do poorly in comparison. When the stress, the effort or the pain are valued higher than the satisfaction that we would get.

By the way, spending money is a pleasure for many people, because the workload as such is hardly included in this balance sheet - and the simple "exchange option" leads to an immediate improvement that increases our well-being (without much effort at this moment).

By the way (the second), there is also an amazing study: We are generally happier at work than in our free time. (I know that seems crazy.) But we have many work challenges that we master - we are needed and receive appreciation or gratitude.

We generate a flow state, experience success and interact with each other. (Of course, this only applies to people who regularly experience these factors at work.) In mental comparison, we often think that work annoys us, but in direct questioning, in the moments of action (at work, as well in our free time), it turned out that we experience more success at work and therefore feel better.

Think about it yourself: How many successes, flow feelings or solvable challenges do you have at work and in comparison in your free time? In our free time we mostly just try to pass the time or get upset about things that happened at work.

Although we actually feel better at work, we often think that we don't feel like working, even though they don't even correspond to reality. However, if we always think about the effort and stress at work (without seeing the success), we create a laborious hurdle of struggle. But if we also take into account all the joys and experiences of success, the flow feelings and challenges that we experience at work, the balance sheet can work better for us here too. Then we feel noticeably better when we focus on the factors that were already there. We just have to be aware of it. So don't imagine the effort of work, but the joys and successes. Back to the topic.

So that this balance sheet can work, our survival instinct is added. Our survival instinct ensures that we strive for satisfaction. We want and need to experience happiness. We need satisfaction for our will to live.

Furthermore, there is no wastage in the nature (of our needs), which means that efficiency is extremely important. Efficiency means: maximum benefit with the least possible effort. Satisfaction must be as high as possible and with minimal effort. And then there's the time span. 200,000 years ago (and also today) people did not want to be satisfied in six months, but immediately and in the foreseeable future (now up to 3 days - which also corresponds to the average amount of food in the household). What will eating help you in six months if you have starved by then? Or what will the water do for you in 4 days if you die of thirst on the third day? Nothing at all.

The brain wants satisfaction NOW - and at all costs. Because only if we always want something in the now can our survival be secured now. The short-term perspective is therefore accompanied by an apparently exaggerated behavior: Who knew when the next drought or famine would come? If there was something in abundance for a short time, it was used as long as possible. In the countries where nutrition is guaranteed today, the effects (from over-eating, lack of exercise, general wastage, etc.) can be seen everywhere. We are biologically designed to strive for abundance.

On the other hand, long-term goals can rarely motivate us. It's too far away. We can imagine it, but there is no direct need NOW. From a purely evolutionary and biological point of view, we are only interested in things that are imminent. This shows e.g. very good at boring things and annoying commitments that we have to make but still have time. We regularly think that we should start now and only when the time is almost over will we do it at the last minute. Then we are motivated by the necessity and take responsibility.

However, if there is no direct need, as with our resolutions (beach figure, general order in life or more activities), it is often very difficult to get active. (For example, athleticism and vitality were necessary to survive before 200,000. Today there are other factors that determine whether we get full. Athleticism is no longer a need for survival.) In summary:

- Satisfaction is a top priority and is used as long as pos-sible (gain pleasure and avoid pain)
- Developed for maximum efficiency (cost-benefit ratio)
- Immediate impact and short-term perspective

= We **now** want **as much as possible** with the **least effort**.

That is the top rule for satisfaction. Building on this, our well-being is assessed. Our actions, reactions, thoughts, worries, needs or problems are based on this "simple" rule. As soon as some of it does poorly: that we have to wait, receive less than would have been possible or have to make an enormous effort (without immediate success), we feel worse. When everything is fulfilled, we feel good and happy.

But very important! Our assessment method and the information with which we compare the circumstances determine to what extent this rule is fulfilled: How do I evaluate the amount, the effort, the improvement, the situation? How do I compare everything? Would I get more or less if I did something different?

Effort and reward go hand in hand, but the usual mindset determines what remains in consciousness. Whether you are disappointed because you were hoping for more or you are happy because you got something is up to you and your usual mindset. The way you automatically rate your experiences determines how you feel. When you worry, you feel worse. If you trust, you will feel better. Of course we can pay attention to our actions or success stories, but in the end it is always the brain's interpretation that determines the way you feel.

In summary, this means that we are evolutionarily driven to do only the bare minimum. We want to get the opium of our body as simple as possible - and everything that takes effort should be avoided. That is the core of life. Nothing more and nothing less - and this becomes very clear in relation to our intentions: New or unusual actions are so difficult for us because the gain in pleasure is uncertain and the effort seems enormous. Even if we want something new, we often don't change anything. There is no need or certainty that it is worth it. However, these factors are extremely important so that we can start at all. Of course, a new activity will be good for us, but the brain also knows that a bag of chips on the sofa will satisfy you - without effort.

50,000 thoughts and 1 wish

We can only change something if we behave differently and act actively. As long as we don't do anything, everything stays the same. I can still wish thousands of times to implement my resolutions, stay strong, or change my behavior. If I don't do something, it remains a wish - pure fantasy. It doesn't matter whether we have an idea or an intention more or less that we don't implement. The only thing that remains are your wishes and your own reproaches, because you cannot realize your (growing) dreams and ideas.

The exciting thing is that we confuse our thoughts with our willpower. We think we want something because it would be nice if we had this or that; But that's not really a "will" that encourages willpower. A wishful thought has the same power as: *"Jabba Dabba Dingdong"*, *"How nice it would be at the sea now"* or *"Hopefully the sun will shine tomorrow."* A wishful thought is no guarantee of strong will:

Of the 50,000 thoughts we have during the day, a casual idea of a wish simply disappears in this mass. It has hardly any substance and there is hardly any motivation because there is hardly anything behind it. There is no path behind it, no goal and no driving force, just the simple thought: *"Oh, that would be nice if ..."*

First, how often do we have these or similar thoughts during the day? We spend most of the day thinking about how nice this or that would be now. It is clear that this will not make us active, but at the same time we conclude that we lack the willpower because we do nothing. Imagine it the other way around. If you had to turn **every** little thought into reality immediately, what would happen? We can be glad that we don't have to implement every thought.

Second, our resolutions or dreams are always an

idea for the future. And at the moment of the idea we are motivated; We have no listlessness in the idea of the future. So the listless feeling after work or the desire to relax because it was a hard day does not exist in the imagination of the future. Our imagination can hardly assume the emotional scope that we experience every day. So it is easier to imagine changes, but it is quite difficult to implement them.

Especially since an idea requires little effort and is thought very quickly, but not an action. We can think of everything, dream of the most beautiful things or activities without doing anything. The idea that we can overcome ourselves is therefore very important. If, in addition to the beautiful goal, I also imagine the feeling of being active after work and how it feels to overcome the listless feeling, then I have overcome myself (at least mentally).

But first I need a clear goal, maybe a plan or a path: If I really want it and regularly deal with it, there are also strong impulses that promote willpower and drive. Then we behave like alone. For this we need an intensive study of the topic, a reason, a "why" - and that is: *"Oh, that would be nice ..."* not. We need something bigger, something better. We need a detailed plan to make this possible.

Why the "why" is important

Therefore, our reason why we want what we want is a very important factor (also for our balance sheet).

When we have dubious thoughts like, *"I don't know how to do it?"* Or something like that, it only reinforces the negative side of the balance sheet.

We have no problem with motivation and also no weak will. We only think it because we may not have been able to successfully implement our intentions or because we believe that an idea is "will" - and it seems to be the same. But motivation and a strong will both arise from an intense focus and our "why" - and we never (or only rarely) deal with our "why".

"If you don't know your why, the "how" doesn't matter."
Igor Gruendl

We have an idea, think again about how nice it would be if we could do it, and then we only deal with the "how": *"How can I do it?"*, *"How can I integrate it into everyday life?"*, *"How long do I need for it?"*, *"How can I do it at all?"*, *"How well can I do it?"*, *"How good is it really?"* And so on. But it's not just the "how". In addition, doubts, questions or uncertainties can arise: *"Is this really the right thing?"*, *"What happens if I fail?"* Or we imagine the efforts and disadvantages that could possibly arise.

These are all "energy costs" that have a negative impact. Of course, some of these questions are important too, but if we just know how to do something, which could be the disadvantages, and even question it (over time) without knowing why we are doing it, then all motivation disappears. Then maybe we know how to do it - without doing it, because we (no longer) know why we wanted it. (And who doesn't know it? Too often we know how something could work; how we would do it - without doing it.)

That's why the "why" comes first, then the "how" - and the doubts have to go away. The "how" usually arises automatically when we actually act (consistently). And maybe we find that we did something wrong or could have done something better, but that's still better than never starting.

However, it is extremely important to find out your own reasons - at least in the long term. External reasons (when someone speaks to us) may be correct, but they can only motivate us in the short term. So it doesn't matter what others say to us or what reasons they could give us. If they don't come from our own desires or don't click in our heads, then they don't have the intensity we need so badly.

Everyone has to find their own why for themselves - and hold on to it - no matter how stupid or naive it may sound. It's less about the realizable or the utopian, it's just about motivating me or not. You need a big "why", a strong belief in your conviction.

The more we think about the personal "why", even in perhaps difficult moments, the more courage, strength and motivation we can generate. Not only our well-being has to submit to the "why", but also our fears or doubts. And they have (partly) great power. We like to start doubting, especially in quiet moments - and that takes strength. Strength that we then lack to act. If something like this happens, we should suppress this dubious thought and act immediately. If there is nothing you can do at the moment, focus on the goal and your why. (Here we need a detailed look.)

Doubtful perfection

As I said, we mostly follow our doubts unconditionally. When did you question your doubts? Or, as Osho once said:

"If you already have doubts, doubt the doubts."

If you constantly question yourself, question your thoughts or behaviors, how could something stable arise in you? How could the strength arise to stand above things? When you make yourself small, small things throw you out of the concept. Your concept should be bigger and more stable. It should be a castle and that won't work if you constantly undermine yourself and your concept. Why do we tend to do that at all? It makes no sense evolutionarily. But if we hardly value ourselves and our performance, it will be clear.

Basically, we think we're not that good because we're not perfect. We don't trust ourselves. We think other people might rate it as "not good". That they could criticize our performance. That they don't see this value that we see. That we have achieved our success through all sorts of things, but not through the value of our performance. It is difficult to assess this value, but we assume that it could be quite good. And at the same time we are concerned that we are fooling ourselves - and that others might notice it.

If we hardly trust ourselves, hardly believe in our performance, it must inevitably come from outside. And then there is the fear that we are not as good as we hoped - the fear of criticism or confrontation. That we are denied recognition or the shoulder tap. That someone does not see our performance as we do. That our worry that we were fooling ourselves was justified. We value others' opinions more than our own. We don't believe in our performance. We don't trust ourselves. We cannot deal with doing something wrong - we want to do it right.

Wanting to do it right is not bad. The only question is who determines what is right? (And why is it so important for us?) If we postpone this decision outside, we are dependent on the "mercy" of other people. We are then victims of other people's opinions - and they often have good comments - comments that we don't have. And if we don't find an answer at that moment, it will damage our own self-esteem. So what can we do?

The desire to always do it right must stop and trust in oneself must arise. We would have to stand behind our performances, whether they were right or wrong. Sometimes they may be wrong, but we would not have to make our entire well-being dependent on it.

What's so wrong with not doing it "right"? Our secret wish for 100% is unrealistic anyway. There will always be people or opinions who see it differently. 100% does not work and does not exist. Free yourself from "100% thinking" and stand behind your performance. Even the best of the best can't do 100%. Perhaps the following thought will help you or as an answer to the next situation: *I'm sorry, but I'm only 80% error free.* A criticism should only get the value it has: a neutral suggestion to learn something. Sometimes it's just about taking into account the needs of others. But the criticism shouldn't be more or less for you.

Ultimately, everyone has to decide for themselves what is right or wrong; and that's enough work. We set ourselves the direction: how we value something and how we act. We decide for ourselves. Everyone sets their own standards. Trust in yourself. You're right. Believe in you and in your convictions.

Hardly anyone tells you (regularly) that you are good; you have to tell yourself. Concentrate on your values and that you "only" represent yourself.

Especially since there is no area in the brain called "self-confidence". There are only processes that create the feeling of being. And we can compare and evaluate this "feeling of being". How strongly it is represented externally, whether it stays calm or creates stress in the event of a conflict.

What fear prevents you and why? Why is it so important for us to do everything perfectly? There is no reason, but if we do that, we will fuel our doubts. Don't question your project, your idea or yourself, but that you have questioned yourself or your project at all. Our doubts are neither a fact nor a reality - and if we look for the origin it will help - and it will also help if we don't know what to do:

Because behind the many big question marks in our lives there are often very simple longings. But we have to recognize them first because our brains tend to think complexly - and we often (automatically) build a huge construct of thoughts, advantages and disadvantages for the simplest desires. In this whole city of desires and desires we can quickly "get lost" and in the sea of possibilities we often don't know what to do. But if we get to the bottom of it and recognize our real motives, it is much easier to find a solution. Then it becomes more tangible for us and we can deal with it better.

Especially since I have to comment that many of our longings, dreams and wishes have a certain price - and we can ask ourselves whether we are even willing to pay this price? So do you research your wishes and dreams and think about what the price would be? How much effort, time and energy would you have to invest? And is it worth it to you? But why is it so important for our habits?

Awareness - an expression of your memories

We are our own consciousness with 50,000 thoughts and 20,000 decisions a day. We are that voice in our heads. We ourselves consist of these 20,000 decisions. That is our nature.

Our consciousness is probably only the ability to actively perceive and change memories. We can specifically retrieve stored information and consciously perceive it. What we call up and modulate creates tangible stimuli to which we can then refer.

Our consciousness is more of a self-perception of the information we remember. As I said, memories consist of emotions and work associatively. Therefore, the type and quality of your memories is critical to your emotional state. As you think you will feel - it works together. A thought is like a building block of memories and emotions. In addition, a thought impulse also releases messenger substances that further influence our feelings. This means that your thoughts also consist of feelings, but can also generate feelings - and we will then perceive all of this.

Perhaps this takes place in the area where memories and perception are linked? Because the memory works so closely with the processing of perception, our memory also becomes perceptible. We can keep this perceptible memory in short-term memory, which gives us an active connection to the (perceptible) information. There we can change or combine these memories, which leads to creative thinking.

We create self-perceivable stimuli, which, in interaction with the entire perceptual and storage process, generate our sense of consciousness. Or in other words:

We can actively perceive our perception process and change this information depending on our associations.

This is different for animals. They can only react directly to external stimuli - according to instinctive or learned patterns. A dog can e.g. also recognize situations or people. What the dog perceives is also compared with his stored information, but he can neither reflect situations mentally nor incorporate this result into his action. On the other hand, we cannot only react directly to external stimuli, but also refer to our own stimuli.

(It is somewhat uncertain whether this is exactly the case, but for me it is the most conclusive. At least that would explain a lot: why we think: "A", say: "B" and ultimately do: "C". We can solve the most complex tasks, compare situations with experiences and act as needed. We can think about the past and learn from it. We can project experiences and actions into the future and even infer a possible future. We have all these skills, but everyone handles them differently.)

So when we think of something, only stored information is called up and modulated - and we perceive these impulses. If we often think in doubts or don't trust our performances, it will show its associative effects. Then future thoughts and feelings are generated in the same way and we have less confidence in our actions; targeted action can no longer take place. Paralyzed by our own feelings, we automatically "bathe" in our suffering instead of acting. It's hardly about the big activities in life, but (again) about the many small ones. That we postpone something, take care of nothing, have no strength or desire to do something, and so on.

This not only reduces our own initiative, but also influences the type and quality of our (routine) actions. We all know that when we are annoyed and have to do routine work. Then we are less friendly (just annoyed) and show no commitment to do the right thing. That is the work of your connection. The action is controlled by the routine, but the thoughts have an associative influence on the feeling. So we can act regardless of our annoying thoughts, but it affects the "quality".

We also don't have to think consciously when we do something. For example, if you have to go to work in the morning, this "knowledge" gives the brain a rough plan that our initiative aims at. Then everything runs by itself. We just "do" without thinking about what we're doing. We get up, get ready, drive to work and think about everything. But what we think then will affect the quality of execution and how we feel.

You can either think or act

Acting and thinking are two pairs of shoes. We can cling to the memories or do something. We can concentrate on the creative change of memories (thinking) or on acting. Our thinking is just retrieving and changing memories. If we focus on this, this process will intensify. However, if we focus on the action, it also strengthens the action initiative. As long as I haven't developed a routine, I can only do one. I can concentrate on thinking or doing something new. Both are activities that use your brain skills. So we prevent us from starting when we think about something.

This process has been studied very carefully in athletes. It is therefore the goal of every competitive athlete to switch off their heads. With equally strong athletes, the art is to stay focused. Mistakes only happen when you think. Or let's take driving again as an example. Every novice driver has to be very focused: blinking, steering and also paying attention to the road. Every experienced driver also keeps an eye on the road, but his thoughts can be anywhere while driving.

Our brain is like a huge information processing device and we act according to the most intense stimuli. These are usually the ones that have arisen from the mass of experiences. If we want to start something new, these experiences are missing and it is difficult to start. Then I hardly have any (stored) information that my new behavior can automatically access.

With internalized activities, on the other hand, there are tons of (stored) information material that can be accessed directly - and than it is pretty easy for us. Conversely, this also means that this hurdle is normal at the beginning. This is the disadvantage of our internalized and routine behavior. This handling of actions ensures that regular tasks are very easy for us because we can do them automatically - we do not need concentration - but compared to routine, it is more difficult for us to take new or unknown actions. Therefore, it is difficult to compare directly with our habits because we compare it with the simplicity of a routine. However, if we no longer compare our new behavior with this simplicity, but instead concentrate on the goal and the action, something changes.

We could also create "artificial" experiences by working intensively on the new. Dealing with the information can also help us if we concentrate on a specific topic in the long term: if we read about it, see something - maybe meet people who already know it, think about our why, imagine the achievement of the goal and so on. Then we create more experience, more information that the brain urgently needs so that we can start more easily.

So make yourself aware of your goals, your why and imagine the success great. Work intensively on the topic. Hang up pictures of the goal or find people who have already reached the goal. Don't think about the efforts, troubles or disadvantages, but think about the laurels, the fun, the improvement; how happy (and with a smile) you make the new activity.

Imagine actively how you overcome yourself, how you overcome your feeling of listlessness. This sense of achievement when you actually get up and start - think about it. Imagine overcoming and the goal.

But the goal can also be to achieve a routine. The priority is not the beach figure, but the regular action. That the (unknown) activity becomes a habit. When reaching the routine is part of the goal, you automatically focus more on the action.

All these thoughts and images are internalized and then serve as an inner template for action. The higher the (mental) experience, the easier it is for you to act. (The mass is decisive again.)

> *"If you always do what you've always done,*
> *you'll always get what you've always got."*
> Henry Ford

We are ready - and we will not be "more ready". Action is the only way to create new routines in the brain that change our behavior in the long term. We only get "ready" when we start. The little resistance that holds us back can always be there. There can always be the voice of memory saying, "No" or "Wait", and the longer we think (or doubt), the more powerful it becomes - and the more insecure we become. But with our attention we can determine what is in our focus.

And if we pay attention to the resistance, it becomes stronger. But if we pay attention to the action, it will also grow. For example, when we go to work, we prove every day that we have to do something and persevere to get something. Of course we have to do it. Or if we want to be sportier, we also have to do sport. The fact remains the same: we have to do something and then we get something for it. We always do something - all our lives. The question is not whether we do something, but only what we do.

Conclusion

We set the standard for ourselves. Our consciousness follows the most dominant stimuli that guide us associatively. The freedom that we mentally ascribe to ourselves is only partially free. The concept of thinking and feeling always follows equivalent thoughts and feelings. This is how we confirm ourselves through our own reactions and associations. And the only way is to think in a new direction so that we can trigger another chain of associations that we can (automatically) follow. The mental direction you use determines your further path.

In the end, everyone can dream, but a thought, a "want" only opens the door for you. But you have to go through the door with an active action. You can have many desires and these can sometimes be fulfilled by luck. But it is always the action that gives you the chance to actually achieve it.

A single thought doesn't change anything - it rots like wood on the forest floor. So take care of the things you want - and start acting regularly. We can and must simply recognize that it will not be easier. We only have the illusion that knowledge provides security. Security that we need so that we dare; that we can jump into the unknown. But we are no longer in school. Knowledge no longer conveys certainty, as it used to be in school, but only keeps us from acting. It doesn't get any easier. Every time we wait, evaluate and think, we move away from the beginning of our action, from our goal.

And if we read anywhere about how to be happy, successful, or relaxed, none of it helps if the knowledge is not applied. Then we are pretty disappointed because everything was promised but nothing works. The devil is in the details. If we only pay attention to the things we want (happier, more successful or whatever) without considering the causes and processes, this will only lead to more pressure and dissatisfaction.

Then we just pay attention to the results and if something doesn't work as we hoped it will be condemned. The greatest danger is too high expectations that we place on our feeling of happiness, our success or the situation. Because we can think of everything so great and beautiful (and promises always raise expectations), they can be so unrealistic - and the worse the disappointments.

We should therefore move away from this "special thinking" and turn to "special acting" so that something changes. First and foremost, the main task is to take action while keeping an eye on the goal - and expectations low. That is the thing that should get our attention.

> *"A man is born to achieve great things*
> *if he can conquer himself."*
> Bruce Lee

That sums it up. Whereby: *"... to achieve great things ..."* is in the viewer's interest: *"... if he can conquer himself."* is the decisive part. We all know what to do. We just have to do it, we have to conquer ourselves instead of distracting ourselves:

> *Growth begins with overcoming inner resistance*
> *and success is the regular repetition of it*

WHAT IS SELF-EVIDENT?

For some reason, many people have an internalized attitude that they cannot be happy, that they cannot have problems, that life must be difficult - perhaps because it was taught them as a child. But nobody can stop us from reducing internal burdens or tackling problems more easily. Only we have this power to ourselves. Nobody points a finger at us and says that we cannot be happy. There is no overwhelming consequence that tells us to hold onto our doubts.

We can only limit ourselves; through our past, through our fears, doubts or worries. We can make it difficult for ourselves if we constantly regret our mistakes or remember stressful situations. Everyone is afraid or doubt - and (again) it's not the big fears. The little fear of being rejected, the fear of failure or just the feeling that you don't dare. The doubts that creep in when you want to do something, or the doubts when you're not sure if it's "the right thing".

It's just so fascinating about things that annoy, strain or scare us. As obsessed, we only think in one direction, find countless reasons why it is so and all clarity disappears. We create a prison of fear that limits us. A prison that we carry in our heads or maybe in our hearts - which has been reinforced by the routines. But in the end it's just our way of thinking: thoughts, opinions and beliefs about lack of courage or lack of confidence in yourself.

The choices you regret in life are mostly "only" those that arose from a lack of courage that we didn't dare. That we didn't take the initiative, didn't say what we wanted, or just didn't do anything. We can blame none other than ourselves.

Note that every limitation, potential, skill or mistake always has the same origin. It is always in your head. And in this mass of decisions, results can arise that we don't always like, that we judge and assess accordingly. But I also have the feeling that most people secretly know this. That they are aware of it, in quiet moments of life. But as soon as we are back in action, as soon as the inner everyday automatism prevails, all of this is forgotten. As if we were caught up in our own routine. Caught in automatic thinking and behavior.

Most of the time we only react to the external circumstances. We react to our fellow human beings, to problems or to our inner needs. When we don't feel like it, when we're angry, or when we're in a bad mood. We react to the beautiful things in the same way: we show gratitude, respect or affection. But mostly people or circumstances have to "deliver" first.

Expensive feelings

It's difficult to be unconditionally respectful on our part, especially when someone is disrespectful to us: *"He didn't deserve this!"*. But why must everything always be tied to conditions? Why don't we act with full conviction, regardless of whether someone "deserves" it or not? It makes no difference to us. It's about ourselves, about the inner feeling, because everyone wants to be liked. Everyone wants to be respected, accepted and understood. Everyone needs harmony, attention and love. (And it may sound cheesy, but if you carry these things in your heart regardless of the outside world, you feel good - but if you make them dependent on behaviors, people, or circumstances, you take away your good feelings.)

Your respect, your passion or your attention also cost no money, cannot wear out and are not limited. And the people who don't deserve this are to be regretted and should not influence our standard. These people can still have so much money, but that doesn't help them. All of these characteristics are included in every person, regardless of their account balance and can be used without restriction -

at least the potential for this would be available.

If you are respectful, attentive, or understanding to other people, even though that person may not "deserve" it, it is not about the other person. Also, don't expect the same from the person. You don't have to worry about it. It is about you, your inner being. That you undoubtedly gave your all, that you stayed true to your standards regardless of the outside world and that the other person had no control over you. (But it also applies to everything else. Everything you do; your commitment, your respect, your passion, you only do it for yourself.)

If you behave respectfully, people will react to your behavior and become (mostly) more respectful. But even if the other one doesn't, if you're not "successful" with it, that person still has the problem - not you. It gets even more interesting when someone insults you and you praise and agree. This confuses this person so much that it is worth seeing the other person's reaction.

> *"You can defend yourself against attacks,*
> *but not against praise"*
> Sigmund Freud

So when you praise the "enemy" you can deliberately confuse them by using and converting their energy. And of course it's easier to write or read than to do it. Depending on the intensity of the opponent, it may even be impossible. Sometimes we just get run over and have little chance, but it helps immensely if we concentrate on the inside.

Why should other people's discontent affect our lives? Why do we give them so much power over us - without getting anything? We don't even get anything for it (except maybe a bad mood) and still give up our power over our feelings. But especially people like that don't deserve it.

There is so much strength and energy in our good feelings and we take it away from ourselves if we (capitalistically) consider it a currency that others should earn. We take our independence, even if we simply give up power over our good feelings. This power should be earned. The power over your emotions should be expensive - not your independence, commitment, or attention.

> *"There is nothing noble in being superior to*
> *your fellow man; true nobility is being superior*
> *to your former self."*
> *Ernest Hemingway*

There will probably always be dissatisfied people. There will always be situations that burden people and can serve as triggers. We also cannot look into the minds of these people. We do not know what their life looks like, whether they are going through a difficult time, experiencing a stroke of fate or simply have never been loved. The fact is, they're just poor. They lack something deep in their hearts and this poisons their entire existence. And in this inner torment and emptiness, they no longer feel so lonely when they bring other people up to their level.

But it doesn't matter because it's about you - and you can free yourself, set your inner self as a benchmark and act independently. Forgive to keep your independence. Think of the love and abundance that you have experienced in your life. Make yourself aware that you are fine - and that the other person has the problem. That he will consciously or subconsciously try to pull you down; that he "wins" if you allow it. But if you don't, if you stay independent and draw your strength from within, the other person can say what they want. Then he has no power over you and most people will notice and stop their behavior.

Forgive such people whether they "deserve" or not. Not so that you demonstrate any "size" and not for the other person, but (again) only for yourself. That you can get rid of it, that you can let it go internally. Because:

What is self-evident?

Nothing in life is a matter of course! We could die tomorrow. The most important people or the person with whom we want to spend the rest of our lives could die tomorrow. And it doesn't even have to be death. We could also lose it because of an argument or because we neglected it. Everything is and remains uncertain and nothing is worse than losing a loved one due to narrow-mindedness or pride.

But the frenzied, constantly repeating everyday life makes many things seem self-evident, which destroy any appreciation and poison your thoughts. Since there is then a lack of appreciation, attentions are neglected, dissatisfaction increases and the willingness to compromise decreases.

The attitude that we take something for granted means that we overlook the uniqueness of life. However, if we stop taking everything for granted, we will see the true values. We need something tangible, and that should never be our routine. We need a meaning in life, a passion, a task that fulfills us. Something we could follow - and if we don't have it - we take our routines. But they are not durable - but what is durable? As an example:

Imagine there is someone who always loves you. He respects all your decisions and accepts your mistakes. That you know you can never be wrong. No matter what you do, he will always stand by you. No matter where you are, he is always with you. You are never alone. He takes care of you and gives you strength. His greatest gift is unconditional love. He will always love and accept you.

Why would the idea be so nice if it really existed? Why can't we be like that and stand for ourselves? Or do we simply postpone this feeling of security because we don't have it within us? Because we had it in childhood and want it back? But we could be like that ourselves. We could remember every day that we love ourselves, that we accept ourselves. That it doesn't matter what we do, that at the time of the action, we always made a decision based on what we thought was right.

We don't have to regret anything because we didn't know better before. (Especially since we can only regret it if we think about the past. There is nothing to regret in our thoughts about the present or the future.) We always choose what feels right at the moment, and if we had known better we would have done it differently. This enables us to unconditionally accept ourselves and our decisions as they were always correct (at the time of the decision). The only thing that should still find a place would be the openness to learn from it (if the expected result is different).

Our decisions and assessments should get less value. It's not about right or wrong, because what was right for us can be wrong for others. If we then insist on our right to correctness, only internal tensions can arise again. But our openness always gives us the opportunity to learn and free ourselves from prejudice. But why are we fighting with all of this? If it doesn't come from us, where should it come from?

It was easier in the past. There were only the gods / the chosen ones or the enlightened and everything happened in their name (or in their philosophy). There was a common thread for life, an instruction manual and an overarching goal. At that time, people could act for it, strive and die. It's more difficult today: what are we doing today? What are we aiming for and what would we die for? We focus on the television program, strive for money and luxury and don't want to die anymore. But it cannot be condemned because this is our freedom. The only question would be whether we are satisfied with it, whether it fulfills us - whether it is the only content or just a bonus? But what gives us the feeling of fulfillment these days? Our everyday life? Our work? Our free time? Our loving environment (maybe the family, if there is one)?

I think that everyone has to find out for themselves and find an inner conviction that they can follow. Whether it is the uniqueness of life, something supernatural, a deep belief in something, love or something else.

Everyone can decide for themselves whether you are the light, a god is the light or whether light is just an electromagnetic radiation. For me it is the uniqueness of life that fills me - and (from this point of view) our life is simply doomed to fail. We will die at some point or at least are not sure.

"Money comes back, but not life."

We probably only live once - and if not, we can't wait until the end to find out. If it continues after that, that would be great, but what if it isn't? As long as we don't know for sure, everything is uncertain, everything is only temporary. Our life is only valuable because it is limited. That is why every day is precious. Life happens now: every second, every moment, every day - not tomorrow, not yesterday, not (only) at the weekend and also not in memory, but always here and now.

> *"The feeling of the moment is always present.*
> *It doesn't start and doesn't stop. It is always*
> *NOW, all our life. Now is our infinity."*
> Renê Egli

But even though we should live in the now, we also need a look into the future. Because one day tomorrow will be today. It is also not ideal to completely supplant the future. Of course, our life is happening now and we also need a look at the present, but the present is not everything. We also need a look into the future, a goal. Regardless of whether we strive for something or take precautions, neither will be successful without thinking about the future. And nobody spends all their money at the beginning of the month because they could die tomorrow. Imagine: if you were to die tomorrow with certainty, everyone would probably do the craziest things, waste their money completely and go through the night. Everyone would get everything out. Understandable, but what if you survived? Those who do not care about the future (because they only want to live now) will find it difficult to achieve goals that require long-term action. So the idea of living in the now is more about becoming aware of the present, but always with an eye on the future. Or rather:

It is a complete package in which every component has its meaning. Neglecting just one thing can have immense consequences: either we don't learn from the past and experience the same problems over and over again. We don't live - and hang in the past or just dream about the future without doing anything. Or we do not strive - no dreams come true and at some point we find that we have missed many opportunities.

Of course, we probably only live once, but we could break away from one-sidedness and devote ourselves to versatility. Balance and harmony are always better than extremes, imbalance or a matter of course.

With a little luck we can grow old; We can go through all phases of life and realize our dreams and goals - from youthful stupidity to the cozy wisdom of an old person. We can take everything with us. We can love, share and laugh. We can be thankful for the feelings that make life so valuable and interesting. We can be thankful for the insecurity in life. That's what life is about. That keeps life exciting. That we have the choice every second to make a decision and not 100% know what the end result will be.

We need the challenge

And even if we turn the tables once, we get the same result again. Imagine a life in which you know your future well. Imagine an immortal life in which all your desires are fulfilled immediately. So imagine a real paradise. Sometimes we wish that and some institutions made a lot of money with it. But if we think it through to the end, we see that it must be pretty unsatisfactory for us.

Because everything would stay the same. There would be no change and everything would be predictable. What would you do in paradise? What quality of life would you have in a completely satisfactory environment that would last forever? An environment in which nothing grows, in which there is no change, in which there is no anticipation, where would the sense be?

Imagine what it would be like to wake up every day and know that there is nothing to do, that there is nothing to hope for, that nothing is worth living because every wish is immediately fulfilled. For a brief moment, you might be satisfied. After a week at the latest, you will get so bored that it would be pure torture. Why do something else? For some people, it is unbearable to do nothing for a week because, for example, they are on sick leave. And that feeling of having to endure forever is more like hell.

And that also applies to life. If there was nothing to do, if everything were infinite ... life would be an absolute ordeal. There would be no courage, no value, no risk, no precious friendship and probably no love either. All things that make life valuable and interesting would have disappeared - would no longer exist.

Fortunately, it is different. So we can enjoy small things or the moment of now, shape the future with hope and learn from the past. Fortunately, there is the moment that makes interpersonal so precious. That is what makes life so valuable. This enables us to experience all the ups and downs of feelings:

The nice thing about feelings is that they are limited in time. This makes them both bearable and valuable.

No matter how bad the day was. The next morning the world looks different again. Then we start anew every day - like a complete life in small format. Our time is simply the most important asset we have, and who doesn't want to have more time, especially on the deathbed? We cannot always fill our time with the activities that bring us fulfillment - we have obligations. But we could learn that we can be thankful no matter what we do. Maybe not for the job, but that we can consciously perceive and experience ... that we live. Try it:

If you have to wait anywhere, take a deep breath and recognize your limited life and enjoy every breath - because you are still alive.

We could recognize and accept that we - and everyone around us - are limited in time. That we have a new day every morning to discover the world. That we have the potential to shape our lives according to our ideas. That we awaken the courage to act. The courage to make mistakes. The courage to live. An Indian story from a show illustrates this very well:

> *"Death is the only wise counselor you have. If you are undecided or don't know what to do, turn to death, your companion. Then you will give up your damned pettiness. Because if death keeps you accompanied, you have no time for stupid thoughts and gimmicks because he can take you at any time. Since any act in my life can mean death, I have no doubt or regret. But since you think you are immortal - and an immortal's decisions can be regretted, reversed, or questioned. In a world where death is the hunter, there is no time for re-pentance and doubt. There is only time for courage and decision."*

Life is too short for a bad mood. Too precious to argue about trifles. Too valuable to ignore the moment. It is your stage on which you are the actor and the director. It is your paper, with your pens, what you can paint. Give yourself a purpose in life that you can be proud of. Give your life a deeper meaning because not much will come from life itself. Do something crazy, something incredible; because somehow we have to pass the time until our death. But be careful - and very important:

Inner change

It's a balancing act - at least in the beginning. Because we can create extreme internal pressure if we want to change too many things too impatiently; especially when our everyday life consists mainly of obligations that we don't like. Then we could judge our situation too quickly because we want to enjoy our lives but the (financial) possibilities or the time are missing. But it's not about denunciation or anything like that. First, it is about accepting your own situation, then looking for improvements within your own options and implementing them.

And that is very important. We cannot change our lives as we might imagine: systems or a functioning organism (like our society) always need structure and regulation; For us, this also means a certain restriction and willingness to compromise. And if we want to use the comfort and technology of our society, we have to "play along". Of course, world peace sounds great without a politics of interest, with a basic income, little work and a lot of free time (to discover the world), but we also have to take into account where we come from (as humanity) or what we have already achieved.

All of our advances are unique in human history. We no longer have to fight for survival. We also need not be afraid that we will starve to death next week. Our shelves are always filled with food from all over the world. We have running water - without the constant danger of harmful parasites. A secure and constant power supply is already part of the basic equipment. We have almost every opportunity to do what we want. Nobody is forcing us. We can change our job, the environment or the country we want to live in. We can shape our lives freely - within the possibilities that society offers us. And if we take a closer look, we are already living in paradise - at least from a biological point of view.

Because all of our basic needs can be met at any time with no risk to life or effort. This is the only way we can take care of other, more complex things. This is the only way we can get upset about little things. Those who have existential problems cannot do it - they cannot afford this "luxury" because they have other problems. And we cannot just claim the luxury of the world without doing anything for it. A hunter or gatherer would have starved to death if he hadn't taken care of his food.

We should make the best of our situation. And maybe we can't change the world, but we could improve our own world - or at least do things that we can influence.

If I ignore acceptance and immediately look for improvements, I can become even more dissatisfied if I (initially) see no way to improve my situation. Changes and opportunities are good, but without accepting the current situation it can get worse. Before we change our outer situation, we should start with the inner one: if I can be happy or relaxed regardless of the circumstances or situations, I can generally be happy or relaxed. It is also not about the latest cars, smartphones or luxury goods. It is about the inner attitude and only when we have reached it can we take care of our external situation. Or as a saying goes:

"You can escape to Africa, but not from the truth."

We always take us wherever we go. We already have discontent in our heads. And our dissatisfaction is rarely related to places, but mainly to us. It is our personal dissatisfaction, to which we have contributed: through our everyday evaluations and longings, which depending on the circumstances deliver a result that can burden us, because we have imagined it differently or did not want to accept it.

Of course, it would be nice to imagine living in a small beach cafe in the South Pacific where everything is as you would imagine it to be. Where you have no more doubts, worries or problems. But this comparison limps. That sounds like paradise again, but how realistic would it be if there was a place where everything was as you would imagine it to be? There are beautiful places and mentalities of different population groups that fit well with your own personality, but that alone is not a guarantee of complete happiness.

Second, we always compare our current situation automatically, especially when it is disturbed - and depending on how we compare, our feeling of stress gets stronger or weaker. Most of the time, however, our comparison is to compare the disturbing circumstance with a better circumstance. This also increases dissatisfaction - because we could be better off if the situation were better.

That means we constantly compare ourselves to hypothetical situations that are better than what we experience effectively. But when I compare much of my life with the best possible situations that I don't have, I rate my life worse and worse because at least in my imagination it could be better. And how can I be generally satisfied when I define large parts of my life mainly through lack or longing?

Like with money

We blame our financial situation for everything too quickly. We think that much of our dissatisfaction comes from the lack of money; that we would be happier if we only had more money. Money may reduce some (money) worries and you can treat yourself to something, but it doesn't make you respectful, balanced or loving. The characteristics that are responsible for interpersonal, professional or general happiness work regardless of the account balance. Your money doesn't matter for the stressful situation, your physical reaction or your patience. It is up to you whether you show respect for people, trust them, have a smile in your heart or appreciate small things.

Money could even make the situation worse because you no longer need help from others. Or that you want to hide your inner emptiness with the account balance and cover it with your pride. That you no longer trust because you are afraid of losing your money, no longer see improvements or no longer appreciate the little things in life.

A large pile of money is power; and this power is more of an enhancer of the qualities that you have. It doesn't change you, it reveals you and your deepest feelings - maybe your inner emptiness. And depending on what dominates in you, whether you can endure unpleasant situations, problems, annoying little things or not; Whether you can value your life or not is much more important for your outlook on life. You won't get rid of your dissatisfaction with a better account balance. They won't go away just because the number in your account is higher. Or as Nikolaus B. Enkelmann once said:

"In the most expensive hotel you can cry the
bitterest tears. On the most beautiful beach
in the world you can feel dead lonely."

And the lottery winners, rich people, stars and VIPs set an example. You keep reading about drug excesses, severe depression, sex / scandals and so on. These people also have fears, concerns, problems or mental prejudices. They also quarrel with the family or feel lonely. (But you only learn about the famous people. You don't read about the people who are not public.) Money alone does not release anyone from his narrow-mindedness. That power is only in you, in the voice in your head. Because one thing is very important:

You are the most important person in your life. After that nothing comes for a long time ... then you come again - and then everyone else comes.

Other people can inspire or help you, but you always come first. You have to get on with yourself. You fall asleep with yourself and wake up with yourself again. Only you need to be able to look into your reflection. It is your attitude to life, your awareness that you are constantly listening and you have to love that voice; you have to love yourself unconditionally - to an extent that no one else has to.

In my opinion, it is always about appreciating your own life and your own opportunities. And if we remind ourselves in everyday life and without pressure that we have so much power with our assessment method, then we could build a new neural highway in the long term and then we will change automatically. Not just thinking that we should enjoy or appreciate more, even in things that displease us, but actively enjoy and appreciate - do it.

And if you had removed all your problems, longings and worries. If there was nothing to fear or hope because everything would be fine ... what's left? Sometimes I have the feeling that we are not made for a life without problems. Our entire evolutionary past has consisted of survival problems. But if you had no more problems to burden, what would happen?

Basically there are only two options: we create problems for ourselves (and we are annoyed by ever smaller problems) or we could be grateful. Gratitude has been preached everywhere for thousands of years, successfully and not without reason. Everyone has something to be thankful for - and in the end there is only gratitude.

A little mind game: what if?

If we imagine for a moment that we would have always decided differently, what would our life be like? How would we be in old age? Looking back, how would we look at our life?

We would have had different experiences, acted differently and decided differently again. Therefore, we would have had different characteristics and different problems, concerns or fears. Our life would have developed in an unimaginable direction - but overall it doesn't matter whether we remember a good experience "A" or a good experience "B" at some point. The fact is that you always like to remember beautiful experiences and then you realize the joke of longing.

That it doesn't matter what we do or don't do. That this everyday excitement and stress will end up in the bucket of time. That it is much more important to be satisfied. Instead of always condemning circumstances, ways of thinking and behavior that we don't like, we could simply be grateful: for our life, for what we have achieved or created - for our daily life, for our awareness and our attitude to life.

We have the ability to find the best for ourselves from the endless amount of information. From the 50,000 thoughts (and 20,000 decisions) we make every day, we could take what gives us strength. The great thing is that you always have your thoughts with you: when you are at the traffic lights, in a queue or somewhere else. You can always think of what you want, what gives you strength, what you can be thankful for. Whether it gives you strength or not is only important for you. And never forget:

> Life always gives you the opportunity
> to do something incredibly stupid.

We can be proud of that. We can trust that blindly. Life does that for you. You don't have to worry anymore. You can let go and concentrate on other things. The opportunities to do something stupid, like something clever, will always come and go. And you will notice some of them - and some not. As I said, I'm not talking about changing your life immediately, quitting your job tomorrow, or flying to Thailand to become a beggar monk. It can wait.

It is an interplay of work peace, house peace and inner peace, but that you work first on your inner satisfaction and then on the external factors. Ultimately, it's about an inner change. That you accept your current situation with all the good and bad sides. That you watch your ratings and values, question your doubts and ask yourself what is real now. When do you get upset? What reviews do you have? What information do you deal with in everyday life? Which neural highways guide you?

And what we do with this information (how we interpret and evaluate it) is up to us. A situation cannot interpret and evaluate itself. A situation in itself is always neutral. Only our mind, which evaluates in advantages or disadvantages, gives the situation a color. But a situation cannot interpret itself and transfer it to us. It's always the mind. Always your voice, your memory pool, what it creates - and the body reacts to it - to the strongest impulses.

The information used for evaluation plays an important role here. Because only the information that we also call up is responsible for the evaluation and interpretation - and this information controls everything else. Behind the everyday things that bother or annoy you are certain information that led to this assessment. So what's your "black spot" hiding in your depths?

As a suggestion: My "black spot" was that I hardly attributed any value to myself and came into doubt too quickly. That my whole effort was often based on compensating for my lack of appreciation for myself. This gave me the pressure to always be better than others (which of course also brought me certain successes). But there was also a kind of compulsion to want to control everything. As soon as I had no control over the situation, I felt insecure. When I realized that for myself, it made me stronger. I cannot control every situation. I have to let go of the need for control. I have to replace the doubts with decisions and simply trust myself blindly. I have to accept the uncertainty and enjoy this feeling as a delightful thrill (like on a roller coaster ride). Now to you:

What is your prison of fear made of?

Which fears influence your thinking and acting? Find out. Observe your reactions, feelings and evaluations: What information has led to this result? What is dominant in your thoughts? What are your strongest impulses and how do you deal with them?

Our fears are self-made anyway. They mainly take place between your ears. In reality, they are not an active threat, they are imagination; Only scenes that we see as a threat or danger that cause the body to generate stress - and only through the body's reaction do our fears - in feeling - become real.

Conclusion

Ultimately, the interplay of body and mind is always responsible for your feelings. The external situation has no direct influence. Our organism is isolated from reality - without connection. Only information to which we then react can be transmitted. It is always the organism that generates hormones and impulses. As long as the organism is not exposed to any real danger and is safe, reality is only a minor matter. But we make it mentally a main thing in which we think again and again about dangers, moments of stress or possible scenarios that make us upset or doubt. In this way we bring all stresses into mental reality and experience them (more often) in our thoughts than in reality.

Our sense of reality is simply a matter of the head because we perceive and interpret it. We don't live in reality. We live in a mixture of perceptible stimuli and memories - and the result is what we consciously perceive.

Your memories, your thoughts, the information you deal with (TV, newspaper, internet, conversations), general stimulus processing and hormone production from the organs, vitality, the nutrient situation, everything is important - everything plays a role in your feelings. We live in a very specific personal self-interpretation that we can feel and perceive ourselves. The reality is there, but we always remain "limited" by our consciousness, by our biology. But that's not bad because it doesn't matter.

We could understand that what we perceive is in our head. That we not only have reality as a perceptible stimulus, but also ourselves. And everything that limits our potential, our fears, worries or self-doubts arises from keeping memories. That we could get rid of it if we let go of the inner voice that complains about everything. Our consciousness is always there anyway - as long as we live and it is always possible to access information from the pool of countless memories that will help us.

Your attention is like a little flashlight in the dark. You can focus on everything - and it doesn't matter what you choose: whether you trust yourself or give up hope, but that will be your way; that will be your feeling. You can concentrate on the bad things or the uniqueness of your consciousness, on your commitment, your trust, on the joys and the love.

The effort is always worthwhile. The struggle always pays off because it is your life - because only you decide whether it was worth it or not. You can decide for yourself - everyone has to deal with themselves. We could reevaluate our fears and develop our strengths and skills so that you become a person who you love and who can tackle problems and overcome challenges. You can move it outside or work on yourself. We also cannot mentally force it because these are effects that only show up over time; if we do something too. There is no pressure either. The only pressure you could experience comes from you. Leave it out and use your focus properly.

The great thing is that we cannot fail at all. If we have big plans or goals for life, it is not 100% safe to achieve them. But once it's all about you alone, your traits, abilities, ways of thinking and evaluating, you can only fail if you stop doing something.

There is no external factor or circumstance that could force you. Only you decide whether you want to change something (in yourself) or not.

You are not responsible to anyone except yourself. Nobody tells you that you cannot be happy. There is no one who prevents us from loving ourselves. Nobody forces you to hold onto your (self) doubts. Only you decide whether you respect yourself or your decisions or not. Only we have this power and can decide and act for ourselves.

We all have the potential to develop. Remember: experience makes life precious. And every second, every moment, we have the opportunity to think about the now and be thankful. This is power that cannot be bought - and it is time for us to implement it: not for others, not for anything, but only for us. For the feeling that we can trust ourselves blindly; that we are right. For our own voice in our heads that accompanies us for a lifetime. That is freedom. It is the greatest gift we have. It is a big event.

"Rediscover the world every day; now and always."

Be simple.

www.ingramcontent.com/pod-product-compliance
Lightning Source LLC
Chambersburg PA
CBHW051457250726
48655CB00001B/463